KT-482-516

Drugs and Violence in Sport

ISSUES FOR THE NINETIES

Volume 26

Editor

Craig Donnellan

THE LIBRARY
NORTHBROOK COLLEGE
LITTLEHAMPTON ROAD
WORTHING
WEST SUSSEX
BN12 6NU

Independence

C602327

First published by Independence
PO Box 295
Cambridge CB1 3XP

© Craig Donnellan 1995

Copyright
This book is sold subject to the condition that it shall not,
by way of trade or otherwise, be lent, resold, hired out or otherwise
circulated in any form of binding or cover other than that in which it
is published without the publisher's prior consent.

Photocopy licence
The material in this book is protected by copyright. However, the
purchaser is free to make multiple copies of particular articles for instructional
purposes for immediate use within the purchasing institution.
Making copies of the entire book is not permitted.

British Library Cataloguing in Publication Data
Drugs and Violence in Sport – (Issues for the Nineties Series)
I. Donnellan, Craig II. Series
362.293088796

ISBN 1 872995 76 4

Printed in Great Britain
at Leicester Printers Ltd
Leicester

Typeset by
Martyn Lusher Artwork, Cambridge

Cover
The cartoon on the front cover
is by Ken Pyne

NORTHBROOK COLLEGE DESIGN + TECHNOLOGY		
602327	Class No 362.293 Don	
MACAULAY	18 Jun 1996	
Location. TV		

CONTENTS

Chapter One: Violence in Sport

Chapter Two: Drugs in Sport

Introduction

Drugs and Violence in Sport is the twenty-sixth volume in the series: **Issues For The Nineties**. The aim of this series is to offer up-to-date information about important issues in our world.

Drugs and Violence in Sport investigates the increase in violence, both on and off the field, and the use of performance enhancing drugs in sport. The information comes from a wide variety of sources and includes:

Government reports and statistics
Newspaper reports and features
Magazine articles and surveys
Literature from lobby groups
and charitable organisations.

It is hoped that, as you read about the many aspects of the issues explored in this book, you will critically evaluate the information presented. It is important that you decide whether you are being presented with facts or opinions. Does the writer give a biased or an unbiased report? If an opinion is being expressed, do you agree with the writer?

Drugs and Violence in Sport offers a useful starting point for those who need convenient access to information about the many issues involved. However, it is only a starting point. At the back of the book is a list of organisations which you may want to contact for further information.

*****

Football and football hooligans

Professional football is by far and away the most popular spectator sport in Britain. Going to football matches is a predominantly male activity, but between 10 and 15% of attenders are female. A higher proportion of the population pays to watch football in Scotland than in the North and Midlands, and the South of England has a proportionally lower level still of paying support (Sports Council, 1986). The Glasgow clubs, Rangers and Celtic, quite regularly attract large crowds of 30,000-40,000 people as do those in the northern industrial conurbations of Merseyside, Manchester, Newcastle and Leeds.

In 1990/91 almost 19 million spectators watched Football League matches. Greyhound racing is the next most popular 'live' sport but it attracts crowds well down on those at football matches.

Apart from a number of small hiccups in the downward trend and a more recent recovery, Football League attendances in England have been in steady decline since the war.

This decline has been offset a little by the rise of a number of knock-out cup competitions and the crowds brought by European club competitions, but there is no doubt that many fewer people pay to watch professional football these days than in the 1940s, and that crowds have fallen fairly consistently ever since that period.

However, in recent years crowds have begun to rise again in England and quite dramatically in Scotland. Total Football League attendances have risen steadily from a post-war low of 16.5 million in 1985/86 to 20.5 million in 1991/92. Around 5 million people are said to attend a football match in England and Wales every year.

There are many reasons why crowds have declined at football in England over the past 40 years. Social habits have changed and there are many more leisure options available today. Households have become more 'privatised' and much more entertainment takes place in the home (e.g. through the role of television and video). Local clubs are not followed these days irrespective of their standing or performances, as used to be more often the case in the past. This, coupled with ease of travel, is one reason why many smaller clubs now have very low attendances. Moreover, the general standards of facilities at some football grounds have arguably failed to keep pace with general improvements in social standards and standards of leisure provision. There has also been criticism of the quality of football now on offer. Some people argue that football is too boring these days and that the game lacks some of the excitement and characters of the past. Players such as Ryan Giggs, Chris Waddle and Ian Wright would seem to provide at least some counter to this argument. All of these factors, however, probably have some part to play in explaining the game's apparent decline in attractiveness to paying customers. However, the continuing strength of the game's cultural significance can perhaps be gauged by the fact that, in 1990 a reported television audience of 26 million people in Britain watched coverage of England's World Cup match v Germany, and that half of these viewers were female.

One thing we have not mentioned so far, but which many people point to in order to explain football's relative decline, is football hooliganism. Hooliganism was not identified as a serious social problem

Figure 1   Arrests at football matches 1986/87–1991/92

	1986/87	1987/88	1988/89	1989/90	1990/91	1991/92
Division 1	2,008	2,216	2,389	1,857	1,747	2,114
Division 2	1,700	2,136	1,747	2,203	1,710	1,328
Division 3	926	866	1,225	1,151	411	1,020
Division 4	878	929	824	734	251	544
All Divisions	5,520	6,147	6,185	5,945	4,119	5,006

in this country until the 1960s – a long time after football's decline began – so it cannot account on its own for football's declining popularity. But there seems little doubt that experience of, and particularly fear of, hooliganism has deterred at least some fans from attending football matches.

Football hooliganism

Although football hooliganism only became recognised by government and the media as a serious problem in the 1960s, hooligan behaviour at football has a long history. 'Roughs' were regularly reported as causing trouble at matches in the professional game's early years at the end of the nineteenth century. Some clubs, sited in particularly tough areas, have long records of spectator disorderliness. In the game's earliest days, local 'derby' matches often provoked the worst problems but, in the absence of visiting fans, home 'roughs' on occasions attacked and stoned referees as well as the visiting players, sometimes chasing them out of town!

Between the wars, football generally became more 'respectable' and crowd problems diminished but did not disappear. It was not until the early 1960s, however, that the media coverage of football began once more regularly to report hooliganism at matches. Around this time, too, there was a general 'moral panic' about the behaviour of young people, sparked by rising juvenile crime rates, uncertainty about the future, the emergence of a number of threatening national youth styles like that of the 'teddy boy', and racial tensions symbolised by the Notting Hill disturbances of 1958. In this climate, football became increasingly identified as a venue at which fights and other kinds of disorder regularly occurred. It was around this time, too, that football hooliganism in England began for the first time to take on the more cohesive and organised aspect that is associated with the phenomenon today.

The mid-1960s saw *ad hoc* match-day alliances being formed between groups of young men drawn largely from local working class housing estates and suburbs. These supporters staked out the goal-end terraces of football grounds as their 'territory' and managed to exclude from them, much more successfully than before, older spectators and rival fans. The development of these 'youth ends' and their role in defending local masculine reputations and territories helped to produce a national network of 'gang' rivalries focused on football. For the young men involved in these groups, their own performance in overcoming or intimidating rival 'firms' began to become more important than the performance of the players they had come to watch.

Today, most serious confrontations between rival fans no longer occur over territories inside grounds. Instead, rival groups sometimes try to meet outside, before, or more usually, after matches. In 1991/92, around 5,000 arrests were made at, League Football matches, an average of 2.4 per match (See Figure 1).

Do only the English produce hooligans?

Far from it. In the early 1960s, the English wanted to pull out of European club competition because of their fears about foreign supporters and players. Today, it is often said that the English export their hooliganism more readily than other countries, but countries like Holland, West Germany, Italy and Spain all have their own named hooligan groups and some even copy the chants and styles of the English. In Hooligans Abroad, some hooligan incidents involving foreign fans are listed. Serious incidents at football matches have occurred in many South American countries as well as in countries such as China and the Soviet Union.

In 1985 English fans were banned from European club competitions because of the behaviour of Liverpool fans before the European Cup Final at the Heysel Stadium in Brussels. A 'charge' by Liverpool fans caused panic among rival Juventus fans leading to a wall collapse and the death of 39 fans.

In 1990, English club sides were re-admitted to European Competitions with no major crowd disorder problems resulting. This followed some disturbances involving English fans in Italy during the World Cup Finals of that year, though many English fans later complained about the policing they experienced in Italy. Opposite are the results of surveys of England fans who went to the European Championships in Germany in 1988 and those who went to Italy in 1990 and who were asked about factors which were significant in contributing to disturbances there.

The hooliganism problem in Germany seems especially acute at the moment given the strains of re-unification and the involvement of neo-fascist groups in football disorder in that country. However, problems involving the English at the European Championships in Sweden in 1992 – which were definitely not caused by overly aggressive policing – suggest that disorder involving England fans abroad has not yet disappeared. England hosts the next European Championships in 1996.

Who are the hooligans and why do they do it?

Most of the evidence on hooligan offenders suggests that they are generally between the ages of 17 and 27, that they are in manual and lower clerical occupations or, to a lesser extent, unemployed, and that they come from working class backgrounds. Unsurprisingly, London hooligans tend to be more affluent than their northern counterparts, and it is 'stylish' and 'macho' in these football circles to show that you have the capacity to spend on, or to steal, exclusive sportswear and that you know which of the available styles are 'in'. Rival fans often judge each other's styles and ridicule those whose dress sense is unfashionable.

Much of the behaviour we commonly describe as 'hooliganism' is ritualistic and non-violent. This involves: verbally abusing rival fans, threatening them with attack, and general horseplay aimed at 'having a laugh'. Core hooligans, however, do seem more interested in fighting or 'running' rival groups who are, in their eyes, like themselves and who are also 'looking for trouble'. Among the reasons they do this is because the prospect of a fight is something which is, for them, exciting and enjoyable.

Furthermore, in the social circles in which they move, the ability to fight, group solidarity and loyalty, plus the aggressive defence of culturally defined areas, are all elements of a satisfying masculine identity (Dunning et al, 1988).

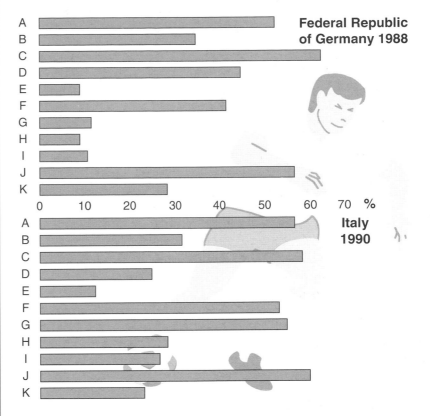

Figure 2 Factors rated by English fans as being highly significant in contributing to crowd problems in:

Federal Republic of Germany 1988

Italy 1990

A Newspaper reports in England before tournament
B Some English fans looking for trouble
C Provocation of English by other supporters
D Drink
E Political groups influencing some English fans
F Cameramen and journalists in West Germany/Italy
G The behaviour of the German/Italian police
H Lack of accommodation of fans in some cities
I Ticket arrangements
J The reputation of English supporters
K English 'patriotism'

Fighting at football is largely about young work-ing class males testing out their own reputations for manliness against those of other young men from similar communities. At matches abroad, English fans often feel they are defending the national reputation for manliness and bravery. That is, they feel patriotic, though often now English fans are the target for attack abroad.

Does drink have a part to play?

In societies like ours, a capacity for heavy drinking is generally recognised to be part of what 'being manly' is about. Males of all social classes are often encouraged, for example, to celebrate special occasions with their male friends by drinking to excess. Football trips abroad, in particular, seem regularly to involve ale fans drinking heavily together in situations where drink, often of an unfamiliar kind, is cheap and easily available. On occasions like this, situations can 'get out of hand' because Englishmen placed in an unfamiliar and perhaps threatening culture have had too much to drink. It does not follow, however, that drink 'causes' hooliganism in any simple sense. After all, many people seem to drink to excess at rugby Union matches, but hooliganism at such affairs is relatively restricted and is often of a different kind from that which occurs more regularly at football. Similarly, hooligans sometimes make a point of staying sober in order better to plot their campaigns. Furthermore, during the 1988 European Championships in West Germany many Danish and Irish supporters were drunk, yet the supporters of those two nations were among the least violent at the Championships. In short, at least some of those young men regularly involved in hooliganism seem to be aggressive in certain circumstances with or without drink.

© Sir Norman Chester Centre for Football Research

It's back – terror on the terraces

Last night's violence at the Ireland v England game has shattered the idea that football has shed its violent image. Football fan Graham Dunbar asks whether we will ever be able to watch the game without fear of hooliganism

Just when you thought it was safe to go back into a football ground...the nightmare returns. It sounds like an advert for a tacky horror film but last night's violence at Lansdowne Road, Dublin, will have mortified true football fans everywhere.

Most people who love the game of football thought the issue of hooliganism was dead. But the sight on our television screens of England supporters once again bringing mayhem to a foreign football ground, squaring up to police as frightened home fans looked on in bewilderment, was a tragic flashback to the 1980s.

That decade was one long chapter of street battles, violence and tragedies at Heysel and Hillsborough with the deaths of scores of innocent people. The 1990s, kicked off by a memorable World Cup in Italy, heralded a new and hopeful dawn and the promise of aggro-free football.

After Dublin many will believe that was a false dawn.

Fans and the game itself have spent the last six years repairing their image in the eyes of a doubting outside world. All seater stadia promised a safe environment for families to return to grounds they had abandoned in fear some years earlier.

A new breed of fans seemed to have reclaimed the game, fans who showed good sense and good humour and displayed their wit and intelligence through their self-written and published magazines, or fanzines.

This spontaneous movement of fans fought for a better deal for the ordinary, football-worshipping, law-abiding fan and appeared to prove to club chairmen and the British game's ruling bodies things had changed for the better and for good.

Dave Lee, former chairman of the national Football Supporters Association, launched in the wake of the Heysel stadium tragedy in 1985, still thinks the gains of the past few years hold good.

> *The sight on our television screens of England supporters once again bringing mayhem to a foreign football ground, squaring up to police as frightened home fans looked on in bewilderment, was a tragic flashback to the 1980s*

'Fans were looking to express themselves through humour and they have created a different kind of fan network. Admittedly the current problems do present them with a big test.'

The new image was celebrated with the cult success of Nick Hornby's 1992 award-winning book *Fever pitch*, a hilarious and moving chronicle of his 25 years as an Arsenal fan.

The book enthralled thousands of readers who would never before have dared admit to being a footie fan or had never before stood on a terrace.

And for the last 14 months comedians David Baddiel and Frank Skinner have given their wacky interpretation of the game in the Fantasy Football League show before an audience of millions on BBC2.

The channel home of middle-brow, chin-stroking cultural studies even devoted an entire night of programmes to witty and oh-so-clever analysis of The Beautiful Game and fans' obsession of it last summer.

A theory grew up that the culture of rave music clubs was finding its way on to the terraces. Teenagers were steering away from alcohol and the aggression it fuelled in favour of the love-thy-neighbour effect of club drugs.

Certainly in recent years I have often seen fans smoking cannabis during games while standing on the terraces at North-East grounds. Somehow we conspired to convince ourselves that things would never be the same again.

We were wrong. As the new season dawned last August, a concert by hot new band Oasis at Newcastle's Riverside venue was abruptly halted when a fan attacked the guitarist and the band fought back.

And the reason given for the initial blow? Apparently Oasis were Manchester City fans and ill-feeling stemmed from that club's match with Newcastle United a few months earlier.

As the season went on there were more and more warning signals; odd incidents at odd grounds throughout the country. Nothing major. Just niggles.

Then came Cantona. Then came Chelsea v Millwall. Suddenly

Then came Cantona. Then came Chelsea v Millwall. Suddenly aggro was back in vogue

aggro was back in vogue. And now comes Lansdowne Road. It is this kind of incident which once more begs the question can football ever rid itself of its minority hooligan element.

There was much hope that the Taylor Report, ordered after Hillsborough, with its recommendations to modernise grounds would inspire fresh attitudes in the game, not least among fans.

One such move saw perimeter fences come down and the opportunity for violent pitch invasions – Maine Road in 1993, the New Den last year, Stamford Bridge last week increase.

The above-named incidents occurred at cup-ties or play-off games where passions run higher, as they will at the European Championships in 1996 when England and its fans will host 15 other nations if last night's violence does not see the competition taken away from this country.

Dave Lee fervently hopes the Football Association will not step back in time. 'I hope we don't see the fences brought back, and that we will all take a sensible view on what has happened.'

But he thinks Eric Cantona should carry some of the blame for the way his karate kick attack on a fan at last month has sparked off a powder keg of trouble.

'I don't think Eric Cantona was condemned enough for something that was reckless and unacceptable. Manchester United have not cut their ties with him, he has been defended by his manager Alex Ferguson and Nike will carry on using him in their adverts.'

When Cantona struck, it was said he was a temperamental one-off and it did not necessarily mean there was a deeper problem.

When Chelsea fans invaded their own pitch last Wednesday after losing to South London rivals, Millwall people seemed to accept such behaviour from those clubs and again it was brushed aside.

Today, the game and its fans cannot afford to be so dismissive.

The nightmare is back…

© *The Northern Echo*
February, 1995

Photo: Sean Dempsey/Press Association

The nightmare is back . . .

Fan's death leaves national game in mourning again

Evil spectre of hooliganism returns with a vengeance as supporter is killed before FA Cup semi-final. Henry Winter says it is time players set an example to curb violence off the field

After riots, drugs and fraud we now have death. What next? The national game faces pernicious threats to its livelihood, the greatest being the deranged mentality of a minority of fans, three of whom were interviewed yesterday following the death of Paul Nixon during Sunday's brawl between Crystal Palace and Manchester United supporters.

The overwhelming majority of football followers remain law-abiding souls, whose conduct is laudable given the passion-provoking environment of match-day arenas. But a sick few represent an evil the game must contain, even if eradication is an impossible dream. Behavioural standards at tomorrow's Palace-United replay (which the FA and police have rightly decided will go ahead) will be closely observed by a fearful sport, particularly in the minute's silence for Nixon.

Complete calm is unlikely. Crowds appear to have re-acquired their volatility this year. The catalysts that activate anger, turning malignant thoughts into criminal acts, range from alcohol, with its capacity for reducing self-control, to perceived injustices during matches, such as player flare-ups or refereeing errors.

The most dangerous cause remains the perception, in the eyes of many fans, that lawlessness pervades the professional game, that a few high-profile players or managers are acting as if above the law. To impressionable acolytes, the logic is simple: if our heroes do not behave, why should we?

The misdemeanours of Eric Cantona, Dennis Wise and George Graham do not in themselves precipitate wrong-doing but they do create an environment where excess becomes almost acceptable. Senior clubs unwilling to censure errant favourites in public are also at fault. Football needs role models not parole models.

> ## 'A sick few represent an evil the game must contain, even if eradication is an impossible dream'

The game's salvation – and there is no long-term reason why it cannot put its house in order – rests with the stars and their disciples. The players have already taken the initiative, however unintentionally. On Sunday night, as a troubled sport tried to come to terms with Nixon's death, the Professional Footballers' Association sent out the right message by naming the clean-living Alan Shearer as their player of the year.

A contrasting successor to Cantona, last year's winner, the Blackburn Rovers and England goalscorer exudes wholesomeness. Shearer's formula, that talent plus hard graft can equal success, is a theme professional football needs to stress to those receptive throngs who take their cue from the stars. Shearer makes a worthy ambassador.

Before Shearer stepped up to receive his award amid much Park Lane pomp, Jimmy Tarbuck urged professional footballers, his 'idols', to smile more, to show onlookers they love a job most fans would do for nothing. These are wise words, which prompted nods of agreement and applause from the game's elite.

Professionals know that a smile is not going to end football's ills but it can reduce tension. Before each

game, however important, it is to be hoped these same footballers think of Tarbuck and smile.

So often, packed houses already seething with internecine rivalry are treated to the ugly sight of well-paid professionals squaring up to each other. Such club-against-club cameos exacerbate the innate competition between supporters.

One source of the Coca-Cola Cup final's success as a spectacle was the patent goodwill existing between the players of Bolton Wanderers and Liverpool. When Steve McManaman lifted up a dejected Jason McAteer at the final whistle, two sets of supporters united. Scarves, not words of abuse, were exchanged.

Like their colleagues, McManaman and McAteer play the game without recourse to challenging the referee's authority, another area where terrace passions can be inflamed. Dissent is a serious problem: what sort of role model is a star who continually questions the officials? The road to chaos leads that way.

If the players have a duty to behave, on and off a field of sport that rewards them so handsomely, so do supporters, who must exercise some form of self-policing. The relative success of the 'hooligan hotline' reflects many fans' desire for action.

The situation would be ameliorated further if the Football Association communicated more with the Football Supporters' Association, who understand the frustrations and potential dangers of terrace life better than Lancaster Gate's committee dwellers.

The FA's officers tread a path through perilous territory. On the horizon is Euro 96, which promises immense profits and kudos. The weekend's events will have disturbed them. It confirms that the hooligan problem is not one England only exports (to places like Dublin, Bruges and Zaragoza), but is alive and kicking at home.

The fear grows that, while the stadiums will be peaceful oases next year, transportation junctions and inner-city drinking holes teeming with young men from differing countries will witness trouble. The sight, on Sunday night, of an M1 service station illuminated by flashing police lights evoked unhappy memories of Seventies and early Eighties mayhem. Those 'no football coaches' signs are understandable again.

The grey area bedevilling the FA is how close to a ground does a public citizen become a football fan and thus their responsibility? The problem is essentially society's; the Government would be well advised to pour extra resources into next year's police budgets.

© The Telegraph Plc
London, 1995

A whole new ball game

Steve Boxer on the success of a system designed to combat football hooliganism

The 1994-95 football season was a draining emotional saga played out as much on the front as on the back pages of the nation's newspapers. While events on the pitch were often thrilling, events on the terraces were sometimes shocking. Suddenly, hooliganism, last seen in aggressive Thatcherite days of yore, made a comeback – most notably at Stamford Bridge after First Division Millwall contentiously dumped Chelsea out of the Coca-Cola Cup, and at Lansdowne Road in Dublin, where an England-Ireland friendly was halted prematurely after ugly rioting.

Maine Road, Manchester City's home ground, was one of many that remained free of hooliganism all season, despite widespread dissatisfaction among City supporters with the team's shaky performance and wild inconsistency. This may be because the local police force, housed at Platt Lane police station, is one of the few in England to employ computer technology to help in its fight against football hooliganism.

The system has enabled officers to keep fans with exclusion orders from entering the ground

---

Platt Lane's computerised system has been successful enough for the local police forces at Manchester United, Rochdale, Stockport, Bolton and Newcastle football clubs to announce their interest in adopting it. It is also a graphic embodiment of the benefits of entrusting database development to those who will actually use the database, rather than to outside consultants.

The system was developed after a successful major operation to arrest a hooligan ring called themselves the Young Guv'nors. CI Wooley, football liaison officer at the time of computerisation, says: 'The intelligence system we had couldn't cope – it was a filing cabinet which no one was using.' Since then, the system has helped to keep organised hooliganism away from Maine Road.

It was developed by Detective Constable Alex Anyakwo. He obtained a standard PC, and developed a graphical football hooligan intelligence database using the humble DataEase Express 1.1 – an off-the-shelf database costing just £275. A scanner, thermal wax colour printer and Toshiba notebook completed the system.

At its heart is a database containing information about, and digitised photographs of, active hooligans and fans excluded from Maine Road, together with details of 'spotters' – policemen acquainted with the database subjects – and known associates. DC Anyakwo says 'The system is constantly weeded under the Data Protection Act; if subjects don't come to our attention for about six months, they are removed.' It is restricted to a hard core of around 100 subjects.

CI Wooley explains how it works: 'Information comes into PC Galloway, the football liaison officer, who screens it and inputs it. On a Saturday morning when there is a home game, we print booklets showing details of fans who have exclusion orders from Maine Road or those who, according to information, may attend and cause trouble. At the back of the booklets are colour photographs of the subjects. There may be up to 300 officers policing the match, from various forces. The booklets go to supervising officers, who typically oversee five or so officers. Officers may jot down information on the backs of the booklets – regarding subjects and who they are seen associating with, for example – which are returned to PC Galloway.

'We also put the latest update of the database onto a Toshiba notebook PC, with a colour screen. The staff officer takes this to the Ground Control Room at Maine Road, where there is a bank of eight CCTV cameras. If he sees anyone doing anything rowdy, he can pan a CCTV camera onto the person and, rather than putting an officer into a potentially hostile crowd, search for that person in the database.'

This helps avoid problems of mistaken identity. Searches can also be performed by entering a detailed description of the subject's physical characteristics.

The system has had some notable successes. Woolley explains that it was even used to trap a suspect: 'We had information that a man wanted for attempted theft, who was a City fan but was staying away from home games, was going to attend an away game. So we took the notebook to that game, identified him and arrested him.'

The system's best attribute is that it enables officers to police games in as low-key a manner as possible

---

The system has enabled officers to keep fans with exclusion orders from entering the ground, but its best attribute is that it enables officers to police games in as low-key a manner as possible – a phalanx of policemen wading into the terraces to make an arrest can have an inflammatory effect on a football crowd.

The success of Anyakwo's budget database system presents the powers-that-be in the police force with an important lesson: a motivated DC with a PC can be infinitely more valuable than millions of pounds of public money. For now, let's just hope that, next time Matt LeTissier gets to parade his skills for 90 minutes in an England shirt, the local police are fighting hooliganism with a system like DC Anyakwo's.

© The Guardian
May, 1995

Courts told to be hard on soccer hooligans

By Julie Kirkbride
Political Staff

Courts will be instructed to get tougher with football hooligans, David Maclean, the Home Office minister, told the Commons yesterday.

The Home Office wants action before the start of the next soccer season when England hosts the European Nations Championship.

Speaking at Question Time, Mr Maclean admitted that only two Britons were banned from going abroad under restriction orders because of convictions for soccer violence.

He said: 'I do not think courts fully understand the powers available to them. They could use them much more fully and better than they currently are.'

He said the Home Office would send out a reminder to all courts on how the powers could be used. The Government was also examining whether exclusion and restriction orders could be tightened.

Max Madden (Lab, Bradford West), who asked the question on restriction orders, said: 'It is extraordinary that the figure has not changed since the riot in Dublin at the Republic of Ireland v England game in February. Does it not show that the courts treat this legislation with contempt?'

Mr Maclean said courts had made thousands of exclusion orders banning hooligans from matches in England and Wales.

© The Telegraph Plc
London, 1995

THE LIBRARY
NORTHBROOK COLLEGE
WORTHIN
WEST SUSSEX
BN12 6NU

Time to combat fascist threat

European MP Glyn Ford seeks a united front on hooliganism

The English are shocked but unsurprised by football violence. For two decades and more, the game here has been punctuated by mass hooliganism. Policemen and fences, videos and security companies have driven it from the pitch and the terraces to the streets. Yet most people interested in football knew it had never entirely gone away.

What came as a revelation last month in Dublin was the knowledge that the violence was preplanned and premeditated. A small group of politically motivated men conspired to organise a riot, even publishing coded messages as to when the violence should be triggered. They were hugely successful. Their aim was publicity and they achieved it.

The violence was organised by an umbrella group, the National Socialist Alliance, which brought together around Combat 18 small regional neo-Nazi groups like the Cheltenham Volunteer Force and followers of the fascist Blood and Honour band.

This infiltration of football is neither new nor peculiar to England. It is just currently taking on a more virulent form as the electoral route to power is seen as increasingly problematic. Back in the 1970s, the extreme right-wing National Front and British National Party used the terraces to recruit and intimidate.

On the Continent there were similar problems. In 1985 at the Heysel Stadium, the Liverpool terraces were littered with BNP leaflets. The Juventus banners were illustrated with fascist and white racist Celtic crosses and runes. The Italian fan who came on to the pitch with a gun was a member of an Italian extreme-right group close to Gianfranco Fini's recently dissolved Moviemento Sociale Italiano.

Similar kinds of supporters are to be found amongst the fans of Lazio and Milan. Paris Saint-Germain are followed by gangs of extreme right-wing hooligans close to Jean-Marie Le Pen's Front National. In Germany, supporters of Die Republikaner and two other neo-Nazi groups recently banned by the German government infest young football supporters.

Their crude nationalism is not against the formation of trans-national alliances. In Bruges two weeks ago, German neo-Nazis carried Chelsea 'Headhunter' visiting cards.

> ### A small group of politically motivated men conspired to organise a riot

The extreme right is making a push to infiltrate football with a new, more violent agenda, pushing hooliganism towards terrorism. 'The Headhunters', a gang who follow Chelsea, are at the front of this missionary activity.

At a European level we need either legislation that will allow prosecution for activities outside the United Kingdom, or a commitment by authorities abroad not merely to wash their hands of incidents by putting individuals back on the boat, but to pursue cases to a conclusion.

The football intelligence unit should take on a European dimension. We already have the European Union's police liaison unit, Europol, based in The Hague, where liaison officers from police and customs units of the 15 members states exchange information on drugs trafficking. They will shortly start to tackle terrorism. It would be appropriate to add the activities of the extreme right and its utilisation of football to further its aims.

The police are in an impossible situation. If rioting occurs they have been too weak and unprepared, as in Dublin. If they control events, as in Bruges, they are accused of violating the civil rights of individuals. Football fans have to realise in such circumstances the police neither can, nor want to, distinguish between supporters who have just been drinking too much and those whose political agenda over-rides any interest in football. The only way to solve the problem is for fans, the clubs and the supporters to act individually and together.

© *The Independent March, 1995*

9

Fair play – the winning way

From the Council of Europe

Sport is governed by a set of rules and, often unwritten, principles of behaviour which usually come under the banner of Fair Play. Sadly, it is often these principles which are not strictly adhered to in a range of sports. The Council of Europe's Code of Sports Ethics is a valuable reminder of the need to demonstrate and practise ethical behaviour in sport.

Aims

The basic principle of the Code of Sports Ethics is that ethical considerations leading to fair play are integral, and not optional, elements of all sports activity, sports policy and management and apply to all levels of ability and commitment, including recreational as well as competitive sport.

The Code provides a sound ethical framework to combat the pressures in modern-day society which appear to be undermining the traditional foundations of sport – foundations built on fair play and sportsmanship, and on the voluntary movement.

The primary concern and focus is fair play for children and young people, in the recognition that children and young people of today are the adult participants and sporting stars of tomorrow. The Code is also aimed at the institutions and adults who have a direct or indirect influence on young people's involvement and participation in sport.

The Code embraces the concepts of the right of children and young people to participate and enjoy their involvement in sport, and the responsibilities of the institutions and adults to promote fair play and to ensure that these rights are respected.

Defining fair play

Fair play is defined as much more than playing within the rules. It incorporates the concepts of friendship,

respect for others and always playing in the right spirit. Fair play is defined as a way of thinking, not just a way of behaving. It incorporates issues concerned with the limitation of cheating, gamesmanship, doping, violence (both physical and verbal), exploitation, unequal opportunities, excessive commercialisation and corruption.

Fair play is a positive concept. Sport is a cultural activity which, practised fairly, enriches society and the friendship between nations. Sport is also recognised as an activity which, played fairly, offers the individual the opportunity of self-knowledge, self-expression and fulfilment; personal achievement, skill acquisition and demonstration of ability, social interaction, enjoyment, good health and well-being. Sport promotes involvement and responsibility in society with its wide range of clubs and leaders working voluntarily. In addition, responsible involvement in some activities can help to promote sensitivity to the environment.

Responsibility for fair play

Involvement and participation in sport among children and young people takes place within a wider social environment. The potential benefits to society and to the individual from sport will only be maximised where fair play is moved from the peripheral position it currently occupies to centre stage. Fair play must be given the highest priority by all those who, directly or indirectly, influence and promote sporting experiences for children and young people. These include:

- governments at all levels – including agencies working with governments. Those involved in formal education have a particular responsibility.

- sports and sports-related organisations – including sports federations and governing bodies, physical education associations, coaching agencies and institutes, medical and pharmacological professions and the media. The commercial sector, including sports goods manufacturers and retailers and marketing agencies, also has a responsibility to contribute to the promotion of fair play.

- individuals, including parents, teachers, coaches, referees, officials, sports leaders, administrators, journalists, doctors and pharmacists, role models who have achieved levels of sporting excellence and those who work on a voluntary or professional basis. Individuals may also have responsibilities in their capacity as spectators.

Each of these institutions and individuals has a responsibility and a role to play. This Code of Sports Ethics is addressed to them. It will only be effective if all involved in sport are prepared to take on the responsibilities identified in the Code.

Governments

Governments have the following responsibilities:

- to encourage the adoption of high ethical standards in all aspects of society within which sport operates.

- to stimulate and support those organisations and individuals who have demonstrated sound ethical principles in their work with sport.
- to encourage the education profession to include the promotion of sport and fair play as a central part of the physical education curriculum.
- to support all initiatives aimed at promoting fair play in sport, particularly amongst the young, and to encourage institutions to make fair play a central priority in their work.
- to encourage research both nationally and internationally which would improve our understanding of the complex issues surrounding young people's involvement in sport and which identifies the extent of poor behaviour and the opportunities for promoting fair play.

Sports and sports-related organisations

Sports and sports-related organisations have the following responsibilities:

In setting a proper context for fair play
- to publish clear guidelines on what is considered to be ethical or unethical behaviour and ensure that, at all levels of participation and involvement, consistent and appropriate incentives and/or sanctions are applied.
- to ensure that all decisions are made in accordance with a code of ethics for their sport which reflects the European Code.
- to raise the awareness of fair play within their sphere of influence through the use of campaigns, awards, educational material and training opportunities. They must also monitor and evaluate the impact of such initiative.
- to establish systems which reward fair play and personal levels of achievement in addition to competitive success.
- to provide help and support to the media to promote good behaviour.

When working with young people
- to ensure that the structure of competition acknowledges the special requirements of the young and growing child and provides the opportunity for graded levels of involvement from the recreational to the highly competitive.
- to support the modification of rules to meet the special needs of the very young and immature, and to put the emphasis on fair play rather than competitive success.
- to ensure that safeguards are in place to prevent the exploitation of children, those who demonstrate precocious ability.
- to ensure that all those within or associated with the organisation who have a responsibility for children and young people are qualified at an appropriate level to manage, train, educate and coach them, and in particular that they understand the biological and psychological changes associated with the development of the child.

Individuals

Individuals have the following responsibilities:

Personal behaviour
- to behave in a way which sets a good example and presents a positive role model for children and young people; not in any way to reward, to demonstrate personally, nor to condone in others unfair play, and to take appropriate sanctions against this type of behaviour.
- to ensure that their own level of training and qualification is appropriate to the needs of the child as he or she moves through different stages of sporting commitment.

When working with young people
- to put as a first priority the health, safety and welfare of the child or young athlete and to ensure that such considerations come before vicarious achievement, or the reputation of the school, club, coach or parent.
- to provide a sporting experience for children that encourages a life-long commitment to health-related physical activity.
- to avoid treating children as simply small adults but to be aware of the physical and psychological changes that occur during maturation and how these affect sporting performance.
- to avoid placing on a child expectations unrelated to his or her capacity to meet them.
- to make the enjoyment of the participant a priority and never to place undue pressure which impinges on the rights of the child to choose to participate.
- to take as much interest in the less talented as in the talented and to emphasise and reward personal levels of achievement and skill acquisition in addition to more overt competitive success.
- to encourage young children to devise their own games with their own rules, to take on the roles of coach, official and referee in addition to participant, to devise their own incentives and sanctions for fair or unfair play, and to take personal responsibility for their actions.
- to provide the child and young person and child's family with as much information as possible to ensure awareness of the potential risks and attractions of reaching levels of high performance.

Summary

Fair play is an essential part of successful promotion, development and involvement in sport. Through fair play, the individual, the sports organisations and society as a whole all win.

We all have a responsibility to promote fair play – the winning way.

© The Council of Europe
March, 1995

The worst attack I've ever seen in football

Trevor Brooking believes United's failed idol is finished in England but says lessons should be learned from a night of shame

Eric Cantona's attack on a Crystal Palace supporter was the most horrendous incident involving a player I have ever witnessed at an English football ground.

It has brought unanimous condemnation from those who witnessed such a ferocious episode and even the most ardent Manchester United supporter must have been shocked and dismayed.

The saddest aspect is that Cantona is a wonderfully gifted talent who has thrilled and delighted us all with his unique range of football skills.

We can ill afford to lose such an entertainer from the English game, but his possible departure is a very real threat now following this latest disaster.

He has continually flirted with danger and his indiscipline has often caused him to figure in media headlines for the wrong reasons.

Manchester United and his manager Alex Ferguson have understandably backed him totally in his past misdemeanours, but they face an extremely awkward dilemma as to how they deal with this latest taint on their reputation.

Crowd provocation is nothing new to football and I doubt whether there is a single player who doesn't experience verbal abuse at some stage or other. Sometimes it can even come from your own supporters when personal form and effort falls below expectations.

This is probably the hardest form of criticism to overcome, particularly for younger players, who can quickly lose their confidence and belief.

It does test the determination and strength of character, and has even resulted in players not fulfilling their potential and drifting away from the game.

Abuse from opposing supporters is generally more derisive and offensive but, personally, I used to find that more of an incentive to improve my performance. I took the attitude that the more they were bemoaning me then the better I must be doing!

> *The FA must act swiftly and firmly to discourage once and for all any such recurrence blighting our game*

Fifa's guide to the new World Cup red card offences

Red card!
Impertinent request by a player to know how much time is left. Immediate red card. Player's bewildered protestations interpreted as offensive body language: further red card.

Red card!
When player wipes sweaty brow with shirt, immediate red card. Offence: indecent exposure.

Red card!
Perfectly legitimate, if slightly robust tackle: immediate red card. Why? No particular reason, except it might encourage wild displays of dissent and lead to further sendings off.

© *The Guardian July, 1994*

If we finished with a successful result, it made the outcome even more satisfying, because I felt it gained you some begrudging respect.

I adopted the same attitude to opposing players as they too often tried to anger or incite a response with some hefty tackling or verbal exchanges.

Cantona's most damaging error as a player is the fact he has shown he will react and revolt against such actions. It makes him a constant target for intimidation and, unfortunately, he seems unable to control his short fuse temper.

Selhurst Park has the players' tunnel near one of the corner flags and so the Frenchman had to walk the length of the pitch after being shown the red card. Perhaps the procedure for players making their way to a dressing room should now be tightened so that the risk of provocation is reduced.

The role of club stewards is another area which needs to be reviewed following this confrontation. Improved training could help them develop the necessary expertise to deal more firmly and efficiently with abusive fans who leave their seats and spoil the enjoyment of other spectators.

The various debates are bound to reverberate for a long time yet, but the indisputable fact is that Cantona has no excuse whatsoever for his behaviour last night. Football has suffered yet another massive blow to its public image and the Football Association must act swiftly and firmly to discourage once and for all any such recurrence blighting our game.

© *Evening Standard January, 1995*

Springboks code of dishonour

Violent play mocks oath to obey rules

By Peter Jackson

The Springboks went into the World Cup armed with a printed code of honour which, one by one, they swore on oath to obey.

All 26 players signed the document, moving the most successful Springbok captain of modern times to declare publicly that there would be no indiscipline.

'I am willing to put money on it,' Morne du Plessis said in good faith the week before the tournament began. Pieter Hendriks' three-month ban last night for punching and kicking a Canadian followed hooker James Dalton's one-month ban for allegedly punching another Canadian.

The fact that too many of the North Americans play their rugby like demented lumberjacks is no defence. The provocation which they employed in general and full back Scott Stewart in particular at Port Elizabeth last Saturday night, was exactly the sort of incident du Plessis had in mind when he drew up the code of honour.

He knew that South Africa had to eliminate the self-destruct element from its rugby if the Republic was to take what the Afrikaaner regards as his divine right at the top of the rugby podium.

The Springboks swore on oath to abide by the rules, that no amount of provocation would deflect them from what du Plessis called 'the biggest journey in all our lives'.

They even went to the trouble of distributing 'a word of welcome' to fans at the opening match. One sentence read: 'As a squad, we seek to bridge the divisions of our past and to soothe old wounds. This has become the new Springbok mission.'

Du Plessis sensed it would be a matter of temperament. 'If we don't have self-discipline, we won't get close to winning the World Cup,' he had said. 'This is not an enforced discipline in which I lay down the law. It's a commitment from each individual.

> *England were by no means totally innocent but the scars took a long time healing*

It lasted for two matches before the schizoid nature of Springbok rugby personality burst into a brawl bad enough for three players to be sent off and five to be suspended. By South African standards, two matches without a single punch being thrown was two more than they had managed during England's tour here last year.

As an exercise in recurring violence, it had to be seen to be believed. England were by no means totally innocent but the scars took a long time healing.

Jon Callard still has his, not surprisingly after the Eastern Province flanker, Elandre van der Bergh, had left the imprint of his boot all around his right eye. Van der Bergh escaped scot-free but then so too did Tim Rodber, although he at least suffered the indignity of being sent off for pummelling an opponent in angry reaction to the Callard incident.

What England experienced, almost wherever they went, was the macho mentality endemic in Springbok rugby: if you can't beat them, punch them, kick them or even bite them.

Against Transvaal, the English lock Martin Johnson was knocked clean out of the tour by one punch. It was allegedly thrown by Johan le Roux, a tough customer who won notoriety in New Zealand later that summer for biting Sean Fitzpatrick's ear.

Le Roux ended up banned worldwide for nine months. James Small, their current World Cup wing,

The Springboks swore on oath to abide by the rules

Photo: Adam Butler/Press Association

was sent off during a Test in Australia for shouting his mouth off at the English referee, Ed Morrison.

At Neath last year, the Springboks took part in a vile match and if the Welsh club wanted a fight, the opposition were more than willing to give them one.

For some, it seems, the code of honour wasn't worth the paper it was written on

---

The real shame is that their rugby is still liable to career out of control despite such admirable figures as the captain, Francois Pienaar, coach Kitch Christie and du Plessis himself. It remains to be seen whether the Springboks can survive the self-inflicted mayhem and still win the World Cup.

For some, it seems, the code of honour wasn't worth the paper it was written on.

Roll of shame

June, 1994: England's Jon Callard requires 25 stitches in his face and head after being stamped by Eastern Province forward Elandre van der Bergh, who escapes punishment.

July, 1994: Springbok forward Johan Le Roux receives nine-month worldwide ban for biting the ear of All Black captain Sean Fitzpatrick.

October, 1994: Llanelli wing Wayne Proctor needs X-rays on his cheekbone after being trampled by Springbok pack.

November, 1994: Springboks accused of provoking infamous free-for-all during Neath game with a head butt.

November, 1994: Accused of sledging and bad sportsmanship by Scotland's Sean Lineen in Districts game.

June, 1995: Pieter Hendriks banned for 90 days for punching and kicking Canadian opponent. James Dalton appeals today against automatic 30-day suspension for being sent off for his part in mass brawl.

© Daily Mail
June, 1995

Writing on the wall for thugs

By Tony Roche

Rugby players will start the new English season staring the price of violence in the face.

The Rugby Union's latest crackdown on thuggery comes in the form of 10,000 colour posters, spelling out the crimes and their punishments and stuck on dressing room walls.

The game's image has been sullied recently through a series of incidents including Phil de Glanville's horrific eye injury, the brawls that punctuated England's tour of South Africa and the recent Johan le Roux scandal.

South Africa's controversial prop was seen to bite New Zealand captain Sean Fitzpatrick's ear and although the match officials didn't spot the incident, le Roux was later banned on television video evidence.

The 'Don't Get Sent Off' poster campaign, led by national referee development officer Steve Griffiths, aims to hammer home the price of poor discipline – with fines ranging from 30 days for punching to life for striking a referee.

England captain Will Carling summed up the players' reaction saying: 'I welcome anything to crack down on violence and weed out thugs.'

© Today, July, 1994

Time to blow whistle on beast within

Rugby union: fight to curb foul play as high stakes result in new breed of violence. Steve Bale reports

The unacceptable fact of violence was clearly demonstrated in South Africa this summer during England's vicious game against Eastern Province. Jonathan Callard (above) suffered ugly facial injuries in the match, while Tim Rodber (right) was sent off after losing all self-control in a pitched battle with Simon Tremain, who was also dismissed. The pair, however, escaped a ban after being judged by their own team managers

Welcome to a new, World Cup rugby season, and if you imagine that the 'amateur' game is overwhelmed – to the exclusion of all else – by the debate about those inverted commas, you would be only part right.

It was Ian Beer, erstwhile president of the Rugby Football Union, who identified the threat to rugby union as money *and* violence, and while opinions differ about the former everyone ought to be able to unite around the eradication of the latter.

In fact Beer, true to RFU form and with some justification, directly linked the two, and the hypothesis that money – meaning the professionalism of the game – would be the root of the evil of violence is a reasonable one. The higher the stakes, the greater the potential for unpleasantness.

The stakes were fairly high when South Africa toured New Zealand and a welter of viciousness culminated in the sending home of Johan le Roux for biting Sean Fitzpatrick –

the sort of ghastly offence that was thought to have disappeared since the pre-television days of 30 or more years ago when some clubs were reputed, only half-jokingly, to have menu cards rather than match programmes.

The stakes, in a purely rugby-playing sense of course, will never have been higher than in next year's World Cup. Rugby's shop-window will never have been more glittering, and so the potential for a metaphorical ram-raid of physical excess which will leave the sport discredited clearly exists.

The International Board has been accused of many things, not least inertia, but under the fresh and

Photo: David Jones/Press Association

thoughtful chairmanship of Vernon Pugh QC it is at least trying. 'Because of the incidents which have been highlighted recently, at the board's interim meeting in Vancouver in October we are going to see what disciplinary procedures should be laid down for the World Cup,' he said.

'We are certainly going to consider what guidelines are to be given to referees to ensure consistency as it relates to foul play, and to make certain that if a player is sent off or cited that the punishment is consistent no matter which country is involved or who happen to be the adjudicators.'

Rugby has not had a foul-play problem at its two previous World Cubs, so this – unlike the crackdown at football's recent World Cup in the United states – is a response to the general rather than the particular, though Le Roux's unsavoury eating habits and England's vicious game against Eastern Province in June have usefully focused opinion.

Then, Elandre van den Berg escaped scot-free after opening up Jonathan Callard's face, and so did Tim Rodber and Simon Tremain when they were judged by their own team managers after being dismissed for punching. 'There has been a concern about what happened in South Africa on the English tour, about Rodber and Tremain being disciplined by adjudicators who clearly had an interest,' Pugh said.

As to the wider question of whether rugby is becoming dirtier, the answer is ambiguous. Fred Howard, who refereed 20 Test matches and is now the RFU's referees' coach, said: 'Domestically, the Courage league has helped in limiting violence, especially with experienced referees who can use that pressure to keep control.

'But in certain areas of the world it has increased. The use of the boot on vulnerable parts of the body in some countries, South Africa being one, and poor refereeing and lenient sentencing have encouraged that trend. How can you justify no action being taken over the Callard incident? How can you justify it to a junior player when two guys are sent off in an England tour match and no further punishment is imposed?'

These are issues the IB will soon try to resolve. 'I don't think a root-and-branch problem exists but at the most competitive levels there is a greater readiness to indulge in a type of violence that we have not, historically, seen in the game,' Pugh said.

'There is more of a readiness and acceptability to cause quite serious harm as opposed to what you can do with your fist.

'In particular, it's the boot to the head in a way that would not have been contemplated or accepted by players 30 years ago. Kicking on the head was a no-go thing then. There is a grave concern, given the damage you can do with your boot, that we should be very hard on someone who does it.'

The issue is more pressing for the IB than merely the World Cup, as a consequence of a House of Lords ruling last year which deemed consent to be no defence to a charge of assault in a case involving sadomasochistic rituals.

There are those who would consider rugby itself a form of sadomasochism but, joking aside, the judgment has serious implications. The Law Commission has since prepared a discussion paper for sports bodies to which the IB, under its barrister chairman, is preparing a written response.

'The traditional view has been that if you were tackled hard and

The boot to the head would not have been contemplated or accepted by players 30 years ago

were hurt, then you consented. That may no longer hold good,' Pugh said. 'If somebody, even acting within the rules, intends to harm another player, that may be sufficient to substantiate a criminal offence.

'It would be beneficial that people knew where they stood. I suspect one of the reasons why we have the current difficulty at international level is not only the intensity of the competition but because there is no absolute uniformity in terms of punishment if someone is seen to be transgressing.

'The Law Commission paper is important because most of the major rugby-playing countries are common-law countries in sports terms and would all be expected to apply similar principles to violence in sport. Rugby is a physical-contact sport which, by its very nature, occasionally boils over. But that is an explanation and not an excuse.'

© The Independent
September, 1994

Security top priority for Euro matches

Action is being taken to ensure violent scenes from the England-Ireland football match in Dublin are not repeated during European championship games in Nottingham.

Security is a top priority as organisers prepare for the event in 1996, Nottingham City Council leader John Taylor has promised.

He spoke out against a growing problem of racism at football matches and in Nottingham during a meeting of the full city council last night.

A working group of councillors, police, football authority representatives and bosses at the City Ground, which will host the championship games, has been set up to look at transport, parking, security, accommodation and tourism.

Coun Taylor said: 'I am pleased to say that security arrangements figure very highly.

'Nazi salutes at a football match, racist attacks on black people on our council estates and skin-head mobs rampaging through the city centre shopping streets are all part and parcel of the same continuum.

'It is a phenomenon which grows because of the economic hardship and alienation which many young people feel.'

He said everyone who watched the 'frightening and disgraceful scenes' in Dublin's Lansdowne Road stadium would fear such behaviour could be repeated in Nottingham.

Conservative councillor John Ryley said he 'deplored' any violence which might have involved the extreme right-wing.

© Nottingham Evening Post
March, 1995

Tragic wish of boxer who put his life on the line for £8,000

Tragic boxer Bradley Stone was fighting for his life last night – his dreams of winning enough money to set up home with his fiancée cruelly shattered.

Just days before his ill-fated Super Bantamweight title clash against Richie Wenton, 23 year old warehouseman Stone told a friend: 'I want to win enough money to buy a house with my girlfriend.'

He stepped into the ring against 26-year-old Wenton for a payday of around £8,000.

But the fight was stopped in the tenth round after Stone took a crashing left to the head, followed by three direct shots to the chin.

He appeared to be fine after the bout, but hours later he collapsed at his girlfriend's London home, suffering from a blood clot on the brain. He was rushed to hospital for an emergency brain operation. Last night he was on the critical list, with his chances of making a full recovery rated 'virtually zero'. He will have another brain scan this morning.

Neuro-surgeon John Sutcliffe said at the Royal London Hospital: 'He is critically ill and something could go wrong at any moment. I

By Christian Gysin, Bill Akass and Geoffrey Lakeman

remain fairly pessimistic in the long-term.

He added: 'Statistically his chances of a complete recovery from this must be close to zero, but you can never be certain.'

'His only dream was boxing – that was all he ever strove for'

Last night Stone's fiancée Donna Lawrence was at his hospital bedside as family friend Peter Faulkner revealed: 'They had just got engaged at Christmas and all they ever wanted was for Bradley to be national champion, to get a title and enough money to buy a home for himself and Donna.

'His only dream was boxing – that was all he ever strove for.

'He was so confident about the fight.'

He added: 'The last thing he was worried about was his fitness – in the weeks leading up to the fight he was as he should be, mean and snappy.'

As a new row erupted over the dangers of boxing, Stone's Liverpool-born opponent Wenton said: 'I am absolutely choked.'

'When something like this happens, a title does not mean anything.'

His trainer Glyn Rhodes said: 'It's a tragedy at a time when Richie should be celebrating his win.

'Now he is sitting by the phone waiting to hear the latest on Bradley.' The secretary of the British Board of Boxing Control, John Morris, said Stone was examined before and after the fight at Bethnal Green's York Hall in East London.

He added: 'He was checked by the doctor in the normal way at the noon weigh-in and obviously again immediately after the contest had finished.

'He appeared to have recovered quickly. He was seen twice more before he left York Hall and, of course, the doctor made a neurological check.

'Everything that was possible was done.'

Hospital consultant Mr Sutcliffe said there should be no criticism of the doctor who examined Stone immediately after the fight, because the boxer seemed to be lucid and was even giving interviews to the press.

'The bleeding from his brain built up over a period of time and Bradley had already walked home before he started to feel dizzy and drowsy.'

Promoter Frank Maloney, who staged the fight, said: 'I feel very deeply for Bradley Stone and his family.

'But fighters are professionals and have bills to pay. Most of them depend on boxing full time.'

Stone, from Canning Town, East London, has been dogged by tragedy in recent months. Both his brother and step-father have died.

© *Daily Mirror, April, 1994*

Box on

By Ian Gibb
Mirror Boxing Correspondent

It is with great difficulty that I defend boxing – for nothing can console Bradley Stone's family.

But I know he wouldn't want it stopped. Of the handful of brave boxers seriously injured in modern times, not one has demanded it be halted.

The best arguments to retain boxing as a sport are the oldest. Ban it and we will end up with something akin to cockfighting or dogfighting.

Driven underground by outlawing it, boxing would then certainly become a barbaric activity.

The vast majority of boxers, amateur and professional, are decent people – taught not only the art of self-defence but also self-control and self-discipline.

We need boxing – as a controlled sport – to stop it becoming a spit and sawdust, eye-gouging, limb-tearing spectacle. The only way to do that is impose strict controls – and let the Government order another inquiry into all safety aspects of the game.

Of course, boxing is basically indefensible. But to ban it would spawn something far worse. And we would be back in the Stone Age.

© *Daily Mirror*
April, 1994

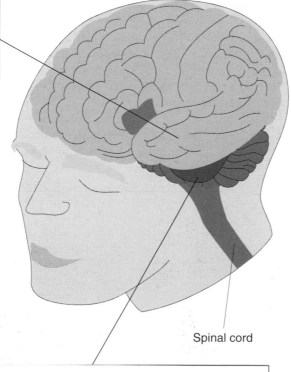

Blood clot the size of a saucer usually at the side of the head

Spinal cord

The blood clot pushes the otherwise healthy brain across the skull and down through the hole where the spinal cord goes. The brain stem is compressed as it is pushed through the hole and you stop breathing.

Ban it

By Jill Palmer
Medical Correspondent

The British Medical Association has called for a total ban on boxing since 1987. This followed a report by the BMA's first working party report on boxing which concluded damage occurred to the brain and the eye in both amateur and professional boxing.

'The major concern over boxing is the brain injury damage sustained cumulatively rather than in any one recorded instance,' says the BMA.

'Most signs of damage are more likely to appear towards the end of a boxer's career or even after retirement.

'Ex-boxers are less able to sustain natural ageing of brain or diseases of brain and may be more likely to suffer Alzheimer's and Parkinsonism.

'Many people think that boxing could be made safer – by the use of head guards or shorter rounds, for example. Evidence suggests that these changes have minimal effect.

'Even the existence of medical specialists at the ringside does not protect boxers from suffering acute blood clots for example.

'The eye is very vulnerable. Damage may result in injury to the retina and possibly detachment.'

© *Daily Mirror*
April, 1994

Why some athletes take drugs

The question of 'why do athletes take drugs?' is difficult to answer as there is little empirical research on the matter, because any sporting competitor admitting drug abuse by entering a research project would more than likely be banned from their sport.

But it is still possible to suggest several reasons why athletes might take drugs.

Will to win

Many élite athletes train full-time – it is their work. They follow special diets, and are supported by specialist services such as sports science and medicine and altitude training. In fact, every support service is available to help them improve their performance, no matter how small the margin. Drug taking is often seen as just another aid to performance.

Pressure

Athletes' beliefs will be shaped by fellow competitors, coaches, sponsors and even the public.

Pressure from any or all of these groups can produce a win at all costs attitude.

Fear of failure

The fear of failure for athletes can be enormous, particularly when set against the pressures to succeed.

Financial reward

Remuneration – either directly through employment, cars or even status in society is just one of the many benefits available to some athletes. Such external pressure can tempt an athlete to gain maximum performance by whatever means.

No single reason can explain the growth of drug abuse in sport over the past 25 years. It is more likely to be a combination of the above factors to varying degrees. But perhaps the single most important reason why an athlete would consider drug abuse is the potentially significant effect on an athlete's ability to train and perform. Unfortunately, this short-term goal may be more important to the athlete than the risk of health problems later in life.

The overwhelming majority of athletes I know would do anything and take anything short of killing themselves to improve athletic performance.
Howard Conelly, the 1956 Olympic hammer champion

The Dubin inquiry, set up after the Ben Johnson positive test in Seoul in 1988, reported that the over-whelming evidence is that anabolic steroids enhance athletic perform-ance. Witness after witness spoke of increased strength and size; a greater ability to train intensively; a better capacity to resist the pain of work-outs, and to recuperate; improved performances; and of new feelings of confidence, physical well-being and enthusiasm.

An athlete's motivation to abuse banned drugs can vary from personal glorification to financial gain. But such temptation must be cast aside since, while sport is open to everyone, all competitors must play by the rules. One of those rules, to ensure fair play and good health, is that competitors should not use banned substances to enhance performance. Drugs should play no part in sport.

• The above is an extract from *Doping in Sport: an information booklet.*
© *The Sports Council for Wales*

Drugs in sport

Drugs and other substances are used by some sportsmen and women to try to do better at sport. The Governing Bodies of Sport, helped by the Sports Council, have introduced measures to make sportsmen and women aware of the dangerous side effects of misusing drugs and to try and stop any unfair advantage which might be gained by misusing them. These measures are called doping control.

A list of banned drugs has been drawn up by the International Olympic Committee (IOC) which most Governing Bodies of Sport adopt. Breaking the doping control rules is, in a sense, no different from breaking other rules [offside, obstruction, etc] as you are cheating against your fellow competitors when you break these rules. You are also cheating yourself and could be putting your health at risk by misusing drugs. As a competitor, you should check with the governing body to confirm which substances are banned in your sport.

This article outlines the different types of banned drugs, explains what they are, why they can be dangerous and gives examples. The classes of banned drugs are listed opposite.

Remember

Using banned substances to try to get better at sport can be dangerous; it is also cheating against yourself and your fellow competitors.

What are stimulants?

Stimulants include various drugs which act on the brain. Competitors may use stimulants to reduce tiredness, to increase alertness, competitiveness and aggression. They are banned because they stimulate the body mentally and physically which may give a competitor an unfair advantage. In addition, they produce harmful side effects.

DOPING CLASSES
- Stimulants
- Narcotic analgesics
- Anabolic agents
- Diuretics
- Peptide hormones and analogues
- Beta blockers
subject to restriction in certain sports

DOPING METHODS
- Blood doping, including erthropoietin (EPO)
- Pharmacological, chemical and physical manipulation

What harm could stimulants cause?

Misusing stimulants could cause:
- a rise in blood pressure and body temperature
- increased and irregular heart beat
- aggressiveness and anxiety
- loss of appetite
- addiction

Competitors have died through misusing stimulants as they make it difficult for the body to cool down, especially when a competitor has been exercising for long periods of time. If the body overheats and is unable to cool down, it dehydrates and blood circulation decreases. The heart and other organs will stop working normally. This can be fatal. Examples of stimulant substances:
- Amphetamine
- Caffeine*
- Cocaine
- Diethylpropion
- Ephedrine*
- Phentermine
- Phenylpropanolamine*
- Strychnine

* Beware – these substance may be found in low doses in cough and cold medications.

If a competitor is found to be using a stimulant, it may be regarded as a doping offence.

What are narcotic analgesics?

Narcotic analgesics are painkillers. They act on the brain to reduce the amount of pain felt from injury or illness and in medicine they have an important use. However, competitors may use them to offset or deaden pain, to mask injuries and to increase their pain limit. Narcotic analgesics are banned because they are extremely addictive and because they make the original injury much worse.

What harm could narcotic analgesics cause?

Misuse of narcotic analgesics may cause:
- breathing problems
- nausea and vomiting
- loss of concentration, balance and co-ordination
- addiction

Increasing the pain threshold may lead to further injury or to permanent damage. Narcotic analgesics can cause physical dependence, leading to addiction.

Examples of narcotic analgesic substances:
- Dextropropoxyphene
- Morphine
- Methadone
- Pethidine

Mild analgesics are found in cold and analgesic treatments without prescription, usually in combination with aspirin (allowable) or caffeine (banned). In small doses, as prescribed by your doctor, these substances are not harmful.

However, if a competitor is found to have misused narcotic analgesics, it may be regarded as a doping offence.

What are anabolic agents?

The anabolic agents class includes anabolic androgenic steroids and beta$_2$ agonists. Androgenic anabolic steroids are a type of hormone known as testosterone. While there are a small number of medical conditions which could be treated with low doses of androgenic anabolic steroids, in sport they are misused to try to make a competitor larger and stronger. For scientific reasons, bigger muscles do not necessarily mean extra strength. Androgenic anabolic steroids may increase aggression which may help people train harder. Competitors misuse them in an attempt to increase strength, power and endurance, to build up muscles and to be competitive. In addition to their therapeutic use beta$_2$ agonists may be used for the same reasons. When given systemically [internally] beta$_2$ agonists may have powerful anabolic effects, hence their use is banned. Examples of beta$_2$ agonists are clenbuterol, salbutamol, terbutaline and salmeterol. Only salbutamol and terbutaline are permitted and then only by inhalation (written notification must be given to the relevant medical authority).

Anabolic agents are banned because using them is cheating. In addition, there could be harmful effects, particularly when androgenic anabolic steroids are misused for long periods of time and/or in large quantities.

What harm can androgenic anabolic steroids cause?

Sportsmen and women may be affected by androgenic anabolic steroids in different ways. As hormone substances, they could interfere with the normal hormone balance of the body and increase the risk of liver disease and premature heart disease. Other harmful effects could include:

In males
- acne
- increased aggression, sometimes resulting in violent and unacceptable sexual behaviour, in the long term leading to impotence
- kidney damage
- development of breasts
- premature baldness

In females
- development of male features
- irregular periods
- more hair growth on the face and body
- deepening of the voice
- increased aggression

In adolescents
- severe acne on the face and body
- stunted growth

Examples of androgenic anabolic steroid substances

Boldenone   Stanozolol
Mesterolone   Testosterone
Methandienone   Nandrolone

Competitors found using anabolic agents have broken the doping control rules and have been banned from their sport.

What are beta blockers?

Beta blockers are drugs used to treat heart disease and to lower blood pressure and heart rate. They could be misused by sports competitors attempting to steady their nerves, and to stop trembling. In particular they could be used in those sports where a competitor needs to keep calm and be relaxed.

What harm can beta blockers cause?

Competitors without a heart problem who misuse beta blockers may suffer:
- low blood pressure
- slow heart rate
- tiredness

The heart may stop because it has been slowed down too much.

If beta blockers are required by competitors who have a genuine medical need for them, a range of effective alternative treatments are available.

Examples of beta-blocking drugs:
- Atenolol
- Oxprenolol
- Propranolol

Beta blockers are prohibited in sports where physical activity is of little or no importance. Competitors who misuse beta blockers and are caught by a drugs tests could be banned or suspended by their governing body (refer to the regulations of international sports federations).

*© The Sports Council
May, 1995*

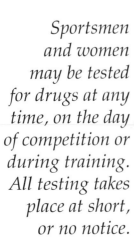

Sportsmen and women may be tested for drugs at any time, on the day of competition or during training. All testing takes place at short, or no notice.

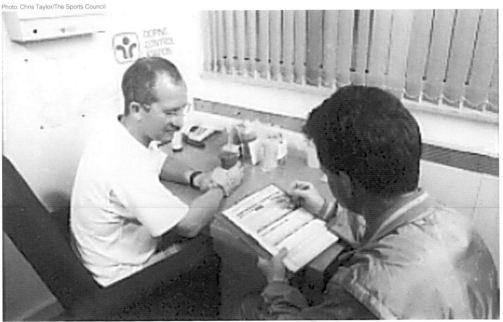

Photo: Chris Taylor/The Sports Council

Doping control in sport

Your questions answered

1 Why the concern about drugs in sport?

Drugs and other substances are now being taken not for the purposes they were intended, but simply to attempt to enhance performances in sport. It puts the health of the athlete at risk. *It can be dangerous.* It undermines the foundation of fair competition. *It is cheating.*

The only legitimate use of drugs in sport is for a medically justified purpose under the supervision of a doctor. Even here, medicines should be sought which do not contravene the drug rules and stand no risk of causing harmful effects.

Governing bodies of sport, encouraged and assisted by the Sports Council, set up doping control to protect sportsmen and women from dangerous side effects and to prevent any unfair advantage which might be gained by cheats.

2 What is doping control?

It is a system whereby urine samples are collected, tested for banned substances and a disciplinary procedure followed if any are found. The aim is to eradicate the use of drugs to enhance performance.

3 Who will be tested?

One cannot know in advance who will be selected for drug testing. Selection is normally made at random on the day of competition or training session. Some governing bodies of sport specify that the winner in each event plus a number selected at random will be tested.

4 How will I know if I am selected?

Sportsmen and women selected for testing will be notified by an authorised official. Those selected will be asked to sign a form to acknowledge that they have been notified and have agreed to go to the Doping Control Station no later than a stated time. Usually you go to the Control Station straight away.

5 Can someone go with me to the control station?

You may be accompanied by an appropriate adult (e.g. your team manager or other official). Usually space is limited so that you cannot bring more than one person with you.

6 What happens at the control station?

The Control Station is a quiet place where the sample of urine can be given and bottled and sealed in the correct way.

You will be asked to identify yourself, the collection procedure will be explained, and you will be asked to:
(a) choose a set of two numbered bottles from those available
(b) give a sample of urine, under supervision
(c) enter on the form any medication you have taken in the past three days
(d) check and sign that your sample of urine has been placed in the bottles you chose, that the bottles have been sealed and the numbers recorded correctly, and that you have no complaints concerning the collection procedure.

7 What if I cannot produce the required sample?

Don't worry, plenty of drinks will be available and you will be given plenty of time.

8 What happens to the samples?

They will be sent to an International Olympic Committee accredited laboratory where they will be analysed.

9 What types of drugs are banned?

The main classes are:
(a) stimulants
(b) narcotic analgesics (strong pain killers)
(c) anabolic steroids
(d) beta blockers (restricted for certain sports)
(e) diuretics

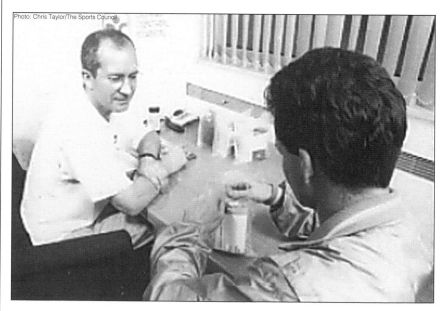
Photo: Chris Taylor/The Sports Council

The competitor will then be asked to divide his/her sample between the A and B sample bottles

In addition, there are a number of banned substances which are not covered by the above categories. A list of examples is available from your governing body. This usually corresponds to the list of examples given by the International Olympic Committee (IOC).

10 *What happens if no banned substances are found?*

Nothing. A negative result will be reported to the governing body of your sport which requested the testing. The samples will then be destroyed.

11 *What happens if a banned substance is found?*

The governing body will be informed that a particular substance has been found in your sample of urine. The governing body will then notify you.*
In general the procedure is then as follows:
(a) you may be suspended from competitions of the governing body while the reason for the presence of the banned substance is considered. For this you* are entitled to:
(i) a second analysis of the urine sample which you* and a representative may observe
(ii) attend* with a representative to present your case.

(b) a decision will then be taken. This may include suspension from competitions of the governing body for a period.

(c) You are entitled to appeal against the decision to an authorised body.

**and your parent if you are under 16 years of age.*

12 *How can I be safe?*

The only completely safe way is to take no drugs. Many commonly used medications, whether prescribed by a doctor or purchased at a chemist's, may contain banned substances. If *medication* is required, you should check every medication in advance for the presence of a banned sub-stance and do not take any medi-cation you have not checked. *Remember this is your responsibility.*

Remember your own doctor or chemist may not be aware of the doping regulations for sport so their view on the safety of a medicine may not be correct. A list of examples of banned substances can be obtained from your governing body to show to your doctor. If you have any doubts, contact your governing body or the Sports Council for further advice.

13 *What if I need medicines for conditions such as asthma, hay fever or other complaints, but am still fit enough to take part?*

There are usually suitable alternative medicines which do not contain banned substances. Your doctor will be able to advise you in the first instance. But remember it is strongly recommended that the composition of the medicine prescribed is checked against the list of examples of banned substances and with your governing body.

14 *How long do drugs stay in my system?*

This is extremely variable, depending on the drug and the individual. Some drugs can be eliminated rapidly, while for others, traces can remain for several months.

15 *Can I avoid detection?*

No – the sample analysis is extremely sensitive; even trace amounts can be detected and identified.

16 *Is it worth the risk?*

No! It may damage your health and your future in sport. In addition, it could endanger the reputation of your sport in this country and abroad.

17 *What if I refuse to take the test?*

If you are selected for testing but refuse to be tested or do not attend the Control Station as requested, it is considered as though the urine gave a positive test. The procedure shown in Question 11 is followed. However, as a sample of urine was not given at the time, there is clearly no chance of a second analysis of the sample.

18 *Couldn't I fill the bottles with someone else's urine?*

No – an official will be with you to ensure that the sample is collected in the correct way.

19 *Why can't I have a list of 'safe' drugs?*

No list will be complete. New medications come on the market constantly. The substances banned are subject to change. The safest ways to check that you are not taking a banned substance are given in Questions 12 and 13.

Note: In most circumstances it is illegal to give any drug to a person under 16 without the consent of a parent. Parental consent is also needed for drug testing in this age group.

Remember – You are the best safeguard of your own well-being, now and in the future. Never put your own health at risk.

NB This leaflet is for your guidance only. Actual doping procedures may vary slightly according to circumstances.

If you want further information see page 39 for address details.

© *Sports Council March, 1989*

I just wanted to get to the top

Two years ago, the shot putter Neal Brunning became only the second British athlete to be banned for taking drugs. As he attempts to start a new sporting career in judo, he tells Mike Rowbottom of the pressures that drove him to cheat

Neal Brunning remembers clearly the moment he decided to turn to drugs to improve his performance. The former international shot putter, who received a four-year ban in 1992 after testing positive for a substance in the steroid category, had just been beaten at an indoor meeting at Crystal Palace shortly before Christmas 1991.

'I thought: "If everyone else can take it, why can't I? If they can do it and get away with it, then let's have a go," he said.

Brunning, who was ranked as Britain's No 2 shot putter in the 1991-92 indoor season, has now given up athletics and is seeking to make a successful career in judo. He is the only British athlete banned for a doping offence who has admitted knowingly breaking the rules. 'I wouldn't touch drugs now,' he said.

At the end of a year when British athletics has announced as many positive tests – seven – as in the previous six years, his comments reveal the pressure and moral dilemma which face athletes in this country and elsewhere.

He began taking testosterone – a male hormone which promotes muscle growth and improves endurance to exercise – in tablet form at the age of 21, soon after competing at an indoor meeting at Crystal Palace on 11 December, 1991. From then until 15-16 February 1992, when he tested positive at the AAA of England indoor championships in Birmingham, he was using the hormone regularly.

'I was taking the tablets every other week,' he said. 'You get them in packets of 60, and I would take two or three at a time when I needed to give myself a boost. I always took the same thing. I didn't get any advice

about what I was doing. I just took the tablets. I thought, "Sod it, if I get caught, I get caught".'

Brunning, a 24-year-old from Lee in south London, competed in athletics for seven years with considerable success before turning to illegal means. Having taken up the discus at 13, he won four English schools titles and three at the junior AAAs. He then found the competition getting too much and decided that drugs had a lot to do with it.

> **'I wouldn't touch drugs now because I know how bad they are and what they can do to you'**

'I did it because I felt others in my event were doing it,' he said. 'It is hard to motivate yourself when you are being beaten by someone who you think is on stuff.'

Drug abuse, he feels, is widespread within athletics. 'I think there's a lot of it going on,' he said. 'I think it's the money. And the ones who put bums on the seats don't get caught. I look at the telly now and see what people are doing and have a good giggle. I see who's getting away with it and who isn't.'

He chose to take testosterone knowing nothing much about it other than the fact that it was a substance which was produced naturally in the body. 'It is very easy to get hold of,' he said. 'Through gyms, and friends of friends.

'I was working 13-hour days as a chef at the time, and then going training. I just needed something to give me a big boost. And it did. The work seemed less hard. I could do a lot more – I wanted to go out and train like a madman. I became more aggressive.'

The health risks he was taking – oral testosterones in particular have been associated with liver cancer – were immaterial at the time. 'I didn't

care. I just wanted to get to the top. I don't think anyone cares if they think there's a chance of doing that.'

Brunning's performances improved when he was taking testosterone. He improved his personal best on three occasions, throwing 17.90 metres and then 18.17 metres – the latter at an international match in Ghent – and recording 18.39m to finish second in the national indoor championships where he tested positive.

Brunning thus became the second British athlete to be banned for a doping offence following the life ban on pole vaulter Jeff Gutteridge in 1988 which was subsequently commuted to four years.

'If you are caught, you put your hand up,' he said. 'There is no point in doing anything else. It just makes you look a fool. That's why everyone still speaks to me – because I admitted what I did and I'm still serving my punishment. I am an honest banned athlete.'

The ongoing case of Britain's 800 metre runner Diane Modahl, whose test sample was said by the Inter-national Amateur Athletic Federation to have shown 'astounding' levels of testosterone, is one which has commanded Brunning's attention.

The level of testosterone is measured by establishing its presence in relation to another hormone, epitestosterone. Normally the ratio is 1:1, but a ratio of 9:1 is admissible in athletics, 6:1 for women.

Brunning's test level was one of the highest recorded – on a par with the 10.3:1 ratio which led to Ben Johnson being banned for life – until Modahl's ratio was reported unofficially at 42:1. Modahl has denied any offence and is currently awaiting a hearing.

'Ben Johnson and I had the highest recorded levels,' Brunning said. 'But now we have been beaten by a woman. Looking at Diane, though, I don't think that result is possible.

'You can tell by looking at someone whether they are taking stuff or not. I just think that it is the way people can race or throw so well so many times in a row.'

Haunted by the past

Like athletics, Neal Brunning's new chosen sport of judo comes under the umbrella of Sports Council doping control, and participants are similarly tested at random in and out of competition, writes Mike Rowbottom

'If people in judo ask me about my past, I tell them,' Brunning said. 'I haven't got anything to hide. That was then and this is now. I am a totally different person. I wouldn't touch drugs now.'

Brunning, who is coached by Alan Roberts at the Dartford judo club, is currently working as a scaffolder and saving so that he can concentrate full-time on judo after Christmas. He is happy to be back in a sport where he reached brown-belt standard as a young teenagers.

'I would have had to do some other kind of sport if I hadn't been able to do judo,' he said. 'I just like to compete.'

Roberts said that Brunning had trained with him for just over a month. 'I know that he is ambitious. He's a heavy man, and he has got potential. If he works hard, he could come through. But it is early days yet.'

Brunning says he is aiming for the 1996 Olympics. That particular ambition is in doubt, however, unless he can appeal successfully through the British Judo Association to the British Olympic Association which rules that Britons banned for doping offences are ineligible for future Olympics unless there are mitigating circumstances.

© The Independent
October, 1994

Two and a half years on from the time when his athletics career was effectively ended, Brunning says he regrets what he did.

'I wouldn't touch drugs now. Because I know how bad they are and what they can do to you. I used to feel sick for a couple of days after I took them. I can't describe the feeling exactly now because I haven't done it for such a long time.

'After testing positive I was told a lot about how testosterone can affect your health and I was worried, so I went to see someone at St Thomas's Hospital who specialises in steroids and had a liver biopsy.'

The biopsy was clear, but it served as a warning. His strongest regrets, however, are for the effect his actions had on others close to him. 'I still get a lump in my throat when I think of how it affected my Mum and Dad,' he said. 'We are only beginning to talk about it now as a family.'

His experiences also contributed to a break-up with his fiancee. 'I was going to get married but that split up,' he said. 'I had been thinking 100 per cent about athletics. I didn't care about anyone else – I blanked them out. And that was wrong.'

The fact that he had cheated, just as he felt others before had cheated, is something about which he is more ambivalent. 'I suppose people would have thought the same of me as I did of others. It just keeps going and going in a vicious circle.'

© The Independent
October, 1994

Today's shame was born from the sins of the past

Dave Moorcroft, the former 5,000m world record-holder, admits that his generation is in no position to preach about the sins of drug-taking

Children playing games define their own rules and consider them sacrosanct. Adults in sport inherit rules and do their best to bend them. Then, those same adults become the rule-makers and conveniently forget their own past misdemeanours.

I can't help thinking that the current drugs crisis is a legacy of a generation – my generation – of athletes, coaches and administrators who now stand in comfortable judgment.

The fact that we need to spend millions of pounds on a world-wide drug-testing programme is an admission of the past failures of a sport that was losing its image of upholding such principles as honesty and fair play.

That failure is now under the spotlight because of the cheating of the 1970s and 1980s. The current generation is suffering as a consequence of the organised abuse of those years.

We may now catch more offenders than before, but I am as certain as I can be that there is far less drug abuse now than there was 10 or 20 years ago.

It's too easy to place the blame on others and point the finger at the old Eastern bloc. But the West also played a major part in the deceit and there are many athletes, now safely retired, who are basking in the glory they achieved through cheating, safe in the knowledge that they now will never be caught.

Those who swallowed the 'go faster', 'throw further' pills did it in a fairly cavalier fashion in the early 1970s and then with greater discretion and, unfortunately, with official protection as drug-testing procedures became more sophisticated in the early 1980s.

There is now considerable evidence that some national governing bodies in athletics either directly organised drug-taking programmes for their athletes or at least protected them from being caught.

Fear is a very effective form of prevention

The cheaters were ahead of the game and showed a contempt for testing procedures. Those were the years when the greatest amount of damage was done as some people in power outwardly portrayed the correct image of concern.

The introduction and development of random testing changed attitudes considerably.

Those who cheated were confident of avoiding detection if they knew when they were going to be tested, but that confidence diminished with the prospect of being tested at any time of the year and without notice.

In 1981, the very early days of random testing, I was competing at a relatively low-key international event which received a surprise visit from the newly formed flying squad of testers.

There was initial panic by some, followed by an outbreak of pulled muscles, strange viruses and disappearing athletes. I learnt a lot that day.

Fear is a very effective form of prevention and random testing has changed so many attitudes.

The thought that an athlete can be tested at any time of the year is a powerful incentive not to cheat.

Random testing acts not only as a deterrent, but has also helped enormously in the drugs education process. Britain, through the Sports Council, has pioneered a system of testing together with a programme of education in schools and clubs that, up until a few days ago, we thought was working well.

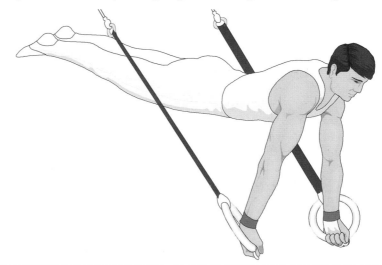

Hopefully it still is, but we have to accept that, as in other aspects of life, there will be the few who attempt to bypass the rules no matter how hard we try to stop them and although testing is a deterrent the real challenge is the effectiveness of the education programme.

We also have to accept that, as testing procedures become more sensitive and the list of banned substances increases, more athletes will give positive tests.

The object of the testing system is to catch those individuals who are taking medications that artificially enhance performance. But there is a considerable difference in the positive effects of the various substances and as a consequence there are varying degrees of guilt.

The taking of anabolic steroids is a cynical attempt to cheat and should be punished severely, ideally with a life ban. However, it is very easy to take one of the lower category substances that are available in over-the-counter medications.

International athletes are given extensive information about what they can or cannot take – aspirin is allowed, for instance, but codeine isn't – but although mistakes should not be made it is possible to get it wrong and produce a sample with a relatively low level of a banned substance. All these offences are categorised as drug abuse, with all the unfortunate connotations that go with that.

This gives an unbalanced picture of the truth and it is important to differentiate between the taking of substances that really do enhance performances and those that are merely a technical infringement. The latter have little or no positive benefit and carry only a three-month ban.

Until the B-test results of Paul Edwards and Diane Modahl are announced, we do not know the extent of their guilt. But whatever happens, it has been a bad week for the image of athletics.

We are only paying the price of a greater level of honesty in the testing procedure, an honesty that did not exist in the world of athletics 20 years ago, when the real damage was done. © *The Sunday Times August, 1994*

History of doping in modern sport

1865 First reports of doping in modern sport
1955 25 urine tests performed on cyclists in one race in France, 5 were positive
1959 Association Nationale d'Education Physique (ANEP) formed a doping commission in France
1962 The International Olympic Committee (IOC) passed a resolution against doping
1963 Council of Europe adopted a clear definition of doping
1965 Professor Arnold Beckett of the Chelsea College of Science and Technology, London University, analysed samples collected from the Tour of Britain cycle race
     The Sports Council formed a working party on Drug Abuse in sport
1966 Chelsea College was responsible for testing samples at the Football World Cup
1968 Drugs testing instituted generally at both Winter and Summer Olympic Games
1969 Professor Raymond Brooks began research at St Thomas's on new testing techniques backed by the Sports Council
1970 Drugs tests first instituted at Commonwealth Games (not steroids)
1976 First steroid tests introduced at Olympic Games
1978 The Drug Control and Teaching Centre established at Chelsea College, University of London with financial support from the Sports Council
1979 The Council of Europe adopted a recommendation urging states to combat drug abuse in sport
1983 The Sports Council called for the expansion of random drug tests in British sport
1985 The Sports Council required that senior governing bodies of sport in Britain introduce drug testing
1986 The Sports Council purchased a Mobile Sampling Unit to enable the random collection of samples at any event (indoors or outdoors) by independent sampling officers.
1987 HRH Princess Anne opened new accommodation for the Drug Control and Teaching Centre at King's College, Chelsea
1988 The Sports Council introduced a revised system of doping control incorporating modified procedures for sample collection in and out of competition using independent Sampling Officers

© *The Sports Council March, 1989*

Athletes sanctioned for positive dope controls during Olympic Games

Games	Country	Substance	Sport
Grenoble '68	None		
Mexico '68	Sweden	Alcohol	Pentathlon
Sapporo '72	FRG	Ephedrine	Ice hockey
Munich '72	Austria	Amphetamine	Weightlifting
	Holland	Coramine	Cycling
	Puerto Rico	Ephedrine	Basketball
	Spain	Coramine	Cycling
	USA	Ephedrine	Swimming
	Mongolia	Amphetamine	Judo
	Iran	Ephedrine	Weightlifting
Innsbruck '76	USSR	Ephedrine	Nordic Skiing
	Czechoslovakia	Codeine	Ice hockey
Montreal '76	Monaco	Amphetamine	Shooting
	Rumania	Fencamfamine	Weightlifting
	Canada	Phenyl-propanolamine	Yachting
	Poland	Anabolic steroids	Athletics
	USA	Anabolic steroids	Weightlifting
	Czechoslovakia	Anabolic steroids	Weightlifting
	Bulgaria	Anabolic steroids	Weightlifting
	Poland	Anabolic steroids	Weightlifting
	Bulgaria	Anabolic steroids	Weightlifting
	Sweden	Anabolic steroids	Weightlifting
	USA	Anabolic steroids	Weightlifting
Lake Placid '80	None		
Moscow '80	None		
Sarajevo '84	Mongolia	Methandienone	Nordic Skiing
LA '84	Japan	Ephedrine	Volleyball
	Lebanon	Nandrolone	Weightlifting
	Algeria	Nandrolone	Weightlifting
	Sweden	Methenolone	Wrestling
	Japan	Testosterone	Volleyball
	Greece	Nandrolone	Athletics (javelin)
	Finland	Methenolone	Athletics (10,000 m)
	Italy	Testosterone	Athletics (hammer)
	Sweden	Nandrolone	Weightlifting
	Austria	Nandrolone	Weightlifting
	Greece	Nandrolone	Weightlifting
	Iceland	Nandrolone	Athletics (discus)
Calgary '88	Poland	Testosterone	Ice hockey
Seoul '88	Australia	Caffeine	Mod pentath (fencing)
	Bulgaria (Gold medal)	Furosemide	Weightlifting
	Spain	Propanolol	Mod Pentath(shooting)
	Spain	Pemoline	Weightlifting
	Bulgaria (Gold medal)	Furosemide	Weightlifting
	Hungary	Stanozolol	Weightlifting
	Canada	Stanozolol	Athletics (100m) (Gold)
	Hungary	Stanozolol	Weightlifting
	Afghanistan	Furosemide	Wrestling
	Great Britain	Furosemide	Judo (Bronze)
Albertville '92	None (522 tests carried out)		
Barcelona '92	China	Strychnine	Volleyball
	Unified Team	Norephedrine	Marathon
	USA	Clenbuterol	Hammer-throw
	USA	Clenbuterol	Shot-put
	Lithuania (1,848 tests carried out)	Mesocarb	Long-jump

Source: International Olympic Committee, Geneva

Test statistics refute charge of a 'drug-ridden sport'

By Mike Rowbottom

British athletics yesterday defended itself strongly against the charge that it is rife with drug abuse. Tony Ward, the sport's spokesman, presented Sports Council figures which showed that more than 99 per cent of all athletes tested in the last three years were drug-free.

He pointed out that athletics had carried out one in five of all tests within domestic sport between 1 April, 1991 and 1 April, 1994. A total of 2,297 tests on athletes had yielded eight positives, leaving 99.96 per cent clean. That left athletics fifth in the domestic standings behind powerlifting (45 positives), weightlifting (16), cycling (14) and rugby league (nine).

Even taking into account the figures since 1 April this year – four positive tests, one refusal and one pending an appeal – the percentage of clean athletes is 99.59 per cent.

'In being tired and angry at the label "drug-ridden sport" given to British athletics, the federation and its athletes are as one,' Ward told assembled delegates from sporting bodies at the Central Council of Physical Recreation's annual conference at Market Bosworth yesterday.

To support his argument, Ward released figures relating to four of Britain's European champions, detailing random and competitive testing at home and abroad this year. Linford Christie has tested negatively 16 times; Sally Gunnell 11 times; Colin Jackson 14 times and Du'Aine Ladejo 12 times.

> ### Sports Council figures showed that more than 99 per cent of all athletes tested in the last three years were drug-free

Since 1974, athletics has had a total of 14 irregular drug tests – four for steroids, five for stimulants, four refusals and one which is pending.

Ward questioned the wisdom, and the practicality, of keeping the names of positively tested athletes secret until a confirmatory test had been conducted on a B sample of their urine. He was heartened to hear news of a proposal to name and suspend athletes after the initial A sample findings which is being made at this weekend's Council meeting of the International Amateur Athletic Federation.

The proposal, which is intended to curtail leaked information during delays before B sample analyses, is likely to be accepted.

Ward's criticisms were also directed within the sport. Referring obliquely to Liz McColgan's reported statements before her comeback race in Coventry last month, he said: 'The cause is not helped when one of our very prominent athletes, as she did recently, talked of large numbers of athletes being on drugs, when she had not the slightest proof what-soever, and who rescinded the statement two days later to "one or two". This sensational type of publicity-seeking does harm to the sport, to fellow athletes and ultimately to themselves.'

© The Independent
November, 1994

Photo: Deutshe Presse Agentur GMBH/Press Association

This sporting strife

Athletes should not be banned from taking legal drugs simply because they enhance performance

By Joe Collier

One predictable outcome of the Commonwealth Games was the scandals about drug taking.

The media – sports pages, commentators and leader writers – have overflowed with righteous outrage, the 'cheats' have returned home under the cloud of orchestrated shame, and the sports authorities have oozed self-satisfied vindication for their policy. The organisers have, as on many previous occasions, defined a sports ethic, and woe betide those found in breach.

However, when it comes to laying down the law, the track record of sport's governing and organising bodies is shaky: why did they forbid full participation by women in so many fields; how could they permit women to be strip searched (sometimes by men) to check gender, what has happened to their stance on payment for taking part in competition? Sadly their current policy on drugs is in the same muddled tradition.

The problem starts with deciding who benefits from medicines, and whether or not this is acceptable. Sports and health organisations jointly promote more active lifestyles, and as competition becomes more widespread inevitably there will be those who have to take medicines to survive, let alone to compete. Drug taking certainly enhances the performance for the disabled or those who might otherwise be ill since, if deprived of medication, they could be no more than spectators. Rightly, these competitors are not breaking rules, but where should the line be drawn? It could be that they are all cheating: what about those wearing spectacles, contact lenses or hearing aids? We have to consider what allowances have to be made in special circumstances, for the competitive embrace increasingly includes the handicapped as well as the gifted. What about the special position of those other entrants who went to the Commonwealth Games – the disabled men and women battling for their medals at many of the same venues? Or the 'Olympic Games' for those with heart, kidney or even liver transplants.

Top competitors can take some medicines, provided they are approved. The problem is that the scheme that has been devised is full of inconsistencies. An élite athlete with asthma can take a beta stimulant, such as salbutamol (e.g. Ventolin) by inhalation but not, it appears, by mouth. However, with enough inhalations the amount reaching the blood is the same by either route. The same holds for inhaled cortico-steroids such as beclomethasone (e.g. Becotide) – inhalation is acceptable, tablets are taboo. Salt tablets are permitted, but not tablets for getting rid of salt (e.g. diuretics). The oral contraceptive is rightly permitted, but there is no doubt it can help a woman with training and competition schedules as it allows for controlled and often shorter menstrual bleeding. Male (anabolic) steroids are forbidden although the unwanted effects listed for them (at least for males) are probably fewer than those for women taking oral contraception.

It may be argued that the sporting authorities have devised their scheme at least in part because they are concerned about the welfare of the athletes. But, if that is so, why should they allow pain-killing injections into a joint which, although offering immediate relief, probably increase the long-term risk of arthritis? Alcohol and beta blockers both steady the hand in precision events such as archery or pistol shooting. Both are effective, but only beta blockers are on the list of banned substances. Should alcohol be, too? And why is cigarette smoking permitted? Smoking is probably the most dangerous drug practice in the world; it is certainly one that alters body chemistry, and it seems most probable that it affects athletic performance.

A parallel issue arises here. Should the sporting associations allow a sporting practice that, by its very nature, causes illness. The athletics world knows full well that excessive training, particularly in young women and girls, causes the bones to weaken. This is a very worrying problem but not one being tackled directly.

The issues involved in the control of 'doping' in sport are not easy to resolve, but the present arrangements do sport a disservice. Their lack of consistency and their failure to tackle the medical and pharmacological issues make the present package untenable. The problem is that the schemes devised have been produced by the sporting associations in apparent isolation, and the implications are far wider than sport alone. There is a need for a group convened by some world-wide sporting authority, perhaps the International Olympic Association, to tackle these issues.

It is important not to leave policy making to bodies responsible for individual sports, or to national governing bodies. Preferably, the code of practice should cover all sports – professional and amateur – in all countries. Implementation alone would be a local matter. We have numerous codes at present and the principle is undermined every time there is an inconsistency.

The group, which should include physicians, pharmacists, lawyers, ethicists, health specialists, and representatives of the sporting fraternity itself, must look for a scheme that is consistent, covers sport generally and can be simply implemented. It must also equip itself to deal with future problems. If a drug was found that could prevent the bone damage in those who over-train, or one that could reduce the rates of troublesome infection in top-class athletes, would these be usable? It would seem reasonable to offer every means possible to reduce illness and prevent future damage, but with current attitudes it is unlikely that such preventative measures would be permissible.

Top competitors can take some medicines, provided they are approved. The problem is that the scheme that has been devised is full of inconsistencies

---

The present arrangements will not do, but whatever scheme is adopted it must be able to cope with at least any immediate developments.

Perhaps the end-point must be the welfare of the competitor. Any practice that might lead to damage would be made unacceptable. Anabolic steroids, which are prescription-only medicines, could be banned because they are not to be used without a doctor's permission. However, they should not be banned because they might enhance performance (this measure might at least reduce the run on illicit trading in impure or defective products). In addition, any practice that was actually illegal could not be contemplated. The use of drugs of abuse, such as cocaine or amphetamines, or opiates for recreational purposes, should be outlawed. But their banishment should be because of their legal status rather than because they might give unfair advantage. The advisory group on drugs in sport will have a lot to consider, but the need for sensible deliberations by a multidisciplinary group is compelling.

© The Guardian
August, 1994

Why I will carry on taking steroids

By Adrian Lee

A bodybuilder told yesterday why he will carry on taking steroids despite the outcry over the death of fitness fanatic James Kevill.

Mark Brown was warned that he is risking his life but he told today: 'I want to compete and if I don't take steroids my rivals will have the edge.'

Mark, 26, from Oxford, is currently between courses. At the end of this month he will begin taking 500 milligrams of testosterone. Over the next two months he will build the levels up to 2,000 mg a week.

The steroids will give him the rippling muscles he needs to succeed in the highly competitive world of bodybuilding. His 14 stone frame will soar to 17 stones. But Mark dismissed the risks.

'I come off steroids after eight to 10 weeks to let my body regulate,' he said. 'I have regular check-ups.

'My doctor knows. He does not approve but he does not preach.'

Ironically, Mark's brother Harold is a big anti-drugs campaigner.

He said: 'I don't agree with what my brother does but it's his life.'

James Kevill, 20, from Southwark, south-east London, died after the steroids destroyed his mind and he butted a wall. Extra aggression is a major side-effect of taking steroids.

'When I gain extra size I do get a bit of aggression but it's under control,' Mark Brown said.

Mark gets his steroids, at £50 for a course, at a gym. He said: 'I reckon about 50 per cent of the lads are on steroids.'

His girlfriend knows he takes the drugs but Mark said: 'She likes me with a bigger body.'

Today spoke to another bodybuilder who takes steroids. He refused to give his name.

'I am not ashamed but my parents don't know about it,' he said. 'I do it to improve my physique, because I want to look good. Without steroids you can only go so far.'

Today gave details of the bodybuilders' steroid doses to David Taylor, clinical pharmacist at London's Maudsley Hospital, where James Kevill died.

He said: 'They're risking death.'

© Today, March, 1995

Testing procedures

A guide for competitors and officials

Testing procedures

Sportsmen and women may be tested for drugs at any time, on the day of competition or during training. All testing takes place at short, or no notice. With competition testing, some governing bodies of sport specify a recommended selection procedure for competitors. For example, new records will only be ratified with a negative test.

Notifying the athlete

After an event or during training, in the UK, the competitor will be notified in writing by a Sports Council Independent Sampling Officer (ISO) that they have been selected for a drug test. Where appropriate, the competitor will be allowed to complete the training session. With out-of-competition testing, the competitor may be given short, or no notice.

Reporting for testing

A chaperone accompanies each competitor to be tested to the Doping Control Station waiting room. Sealed, non-alcoholic drinks are available, alongside reading material. All competitors are entitled to have a representative (from the sport's national governing body) present.

Selecting a collection vessel

When the competitor is ready to provide a sample of urine, he/she is asked to select a sample collection vessel.

Providing a sample under supervision

The competitor must remove sufficient clothing so that the ISO can directly observe the competitor providing the urine sample into the collection vessel. When the competitor has provided the required amount of urine – generally 100 ml – he/she must return directly to the Doping Control Station admin-

istration room. Only the competitor should handle the sample.

Selecting the sample containers

The competitor will now be asked to select a pair of pre-sealed bottle containers.

Breaking the security seals

The competitor will be invited to break the security seals.

Dividing the sample

The competitor will then be asked to divide the sample between the A and B sample bottles, putting approximately two-thirds of the sample into the A bottle and a minimum of 30 ml into the B bottle.

Sealing the samples

The ISO ensures that the bottles have been tightly sealed by checking

---

Competitors can, of course, refuse to be tested. However, such a refusal is considered as though the urine sample gave a positive result

---

the bottle tops. The competitor is then invited to select two numbered seals and to seal the A and B packs.

Recording the information

The ISO records the bottle code and seal numbers on the Doping Control Collection Form: this information is checked by the competitor. The competitor is then asked to declare any medications that have been taken in the previous week.

Certifying the information

The ISO then asks the competitor (and their representative if present) to check all the information on the Drug Control Collection Form and if satisfied, to sign the form. The ISO will also check and sign the form. The ISO provides the competitor with a copy of the Doping Control Collection Form and the competitor is free to go.

Transferring the samples to the laboratory

The samples – in their sealed transit containers – are then sent to an accredited laboratory by a secure chain of custody for analysis. The laboratory receives the copy of the Doping Control Collection Form which details only the sample, seal numbers and the competitor's medications. No other information is provided which might allow the competitor to be identified.

Reporting the analytical result

Following laboratory analysis of the competitor's A sample, if no banned substances are found, a negative result will be reported to the relevant sport governing body and the B sample destroyed. This report is usually available within 10 days of the sample collection. If required, results can be made available within 24 hours during a

major competition. If banned substances are found, the governing body is notified of the finding. The governing body then notifies the competitor.

In the case of a positive test, the procedure is generally as follows:

a) the competitor may be suspended from competition while the reason for the presence of the banned substance is considered.

The competitor is then entitled to a second analysis of the urine sample in the B bottle which the competitor (and/or a representative) may observe, plus an opportunity to present his/her case.

b) a decision will be taken. This may include suspension from competition for a given period, or even in some cases, a lifetime ban.

c) every competitor is, however, entitled to appeal against the decision reached.

These procedures have been developed to ensure security and fairness in drug testing. Competitors can, of course, refuse to be tested. However, such a refusal is considered as though the urine sample gave a positive result.
(A detailed list of the classes of drugs which are banned by the International Olympic Committee (IOC) is available from the Sports Council. Those 'over the counter' preparations which may be taken for common ailments (such as hayfever, asthma, etc) and which are permitted under the doping regulations of the IOC are listed in the Sports Council's Doping Control information booklet, number 4.)

© The Sports Council

UK legislation on doping substances in sport

Introduction

Presently, there is no specific legislation controlling the use of drugs in sport in the UK. However, many of the doping substances included in the International Olympic Committee's list of Doping Classes are controlled under general legislation concerned with the control of drugs, the Misuse of Drugs Act 1971 and the Medicines Act 1968.

A summary of the legislation and its application to doping substances used in sport is given below.

Misuse of Drugs Act 1971

This Act replaced the Dangerous Drugs Acts of 1965 and 1967 and Drugs (Prevention of Misuse) Act 1964.

It provides powers to prevent the misuse of drugs, and to deal with social problems related to their misuse in several ways. It establishes a list of all dangerous or otherwise harmful substances and products, that is, controlled drugs, and creates a framework to prevent their misuse. This framework involves restrictions and controls on the import, export, production, supply and possession of controlled drugs; safe custody, licensing, regulating of prescriptions, power to withdraw authority from doctors, dentists, veterinary surgeons or pharmacists and the punishment of offenders.

Controlled drugs are listed in Schedule 2 of the Misuse of Drugs Act 1971 and are divided into three classes: A, B and C. The classification is used to determine the penalties which may be imposed for offences involving drug misuse.

Enforcement of the Act is the responsibility of the Home Office through the Police and the Courts.

Misuse of Drugs Regulations 1985

These Regulations apply regimes of control to controlled drugs which have been specified in Schedule 1 to 5 of the Regulations. Schedule 1 lists certain drugs which are mainly, with one exception, not used for therapeutic purposes in the UK and which are not generally available. Possession and supply is subject to licence granted by the Home Secretary, and their use is limited almost entirely to research. Schedule 2 lists drugs in medical use which are regarded as particularly dangerous if misused. Schedules 3 and 4 list certain drugs which are regarded as less dangerous. Further regulations govern the production, supply and possession of controlled drugs and documentation of supplies including prescriptions.

Medicines Act 1968

This Act provides for the control of medicinal products and substances through a system of licences, including the licensing of firms engaged in their manufacture or wholesale. There are three categories of status of the products controlled under the Medicines Act 1968 which, dependent upon the ingredients involved, govern the availability of medicines:
(a) The Prescription Only Medicines (POM) list where products may only be provided on a prescription from a medical practitioner.
(b) The General Sales List (GSL) where products may be purchased over the counter.

(c) Medicines whose ingredients are not covered by the POM or GSL lists, are pharmacy only and may only be sold under a pharmacist's supervision.

Specifically, a product licence is needed to market or import a medicine; manufacturers' and wholesale dealers' licences are needed for these operations.

Enforcement of the Medicines Act is the responsibility of the Department of Health.

Application of legislation to the IOC list of Doping Classes

The IOC list of Doping Classes (March 1993) includes the following classes:

Doping classes
(a) Stimulants
(b) Narcotics
(c) Anabolic agents
(d) Diuretics
(e) Peptide hormones and analogues

Classes of drugs subject to certain restrictions
(a) Alcohol
(b) Marijuana
(c) Local Anaesthetics
(d) Corticosteroids
(e) Beta blockers

All substances listed in Classes ID, E and IIIC, D and E appear in the POM order and all those substances listed in Class IB are either covered by the POM order or the Misuse of Drugs Act.

Most of the substances in Classes IA and IC are covered by either statute but caffeine appears on GSL of the Medicines Act 1968. However, there are approximately ten substances for which there is no control under the Medicines Act because they are not ingredients in licensed medicines. These include the anabolic steroids: Bolasterone, Boldenone, Chlordehydromethyltestosterone and Methenolone.

Specific application to anabolic steroids

Unlicensed dealing in, selling and/or supplying, and obtaining of anabolic steroids without a licence are offences against the Medicines Act 1968. Offences would be liable to criminal proceedings and could attract penalties of fines and/or imprisonment. For example, unlicensed trading on summary conviction could attract a fine not exceeding £2,000; on conviction of indictment, higher penalties, including imprisonment, could be imposed.

The Medicines Act 1968 does not control the abuse of anabolic steroids or other substances. Possession of anabolic steroids does not constitute an offence under the Act.

Prosecutions

Since October 1986, there have been ten successful prosecutions under the Medicines Act 1968 for the illegal sale of anabolic steroids, generally resulting in fines and/or imprisonment.

© The Sports Council Doping Control Unit

What is banned?

From The Sports Council for Wales

Athletes, of course, suffer from illnesses and are prone to develop muscular and skeletal injuries. It is vital, therefore, that clear guidance is given to athletes, so that they are aware of what they can and cannot take.

The whole subject of what is and is not banned is still a problem for both the IOC Medical Committee, which specifies the banned classes, and sports administrators, many of whom have little experience of dealing with such complicated issues.

Most governing bodies accept the IOC recommendations. A key difficulty is updating information when so many new drugs come onto the market and existing ones are withdrawn. It is difficult, therefore, to keep athletes fully up to date with the latest information.

The IOC goes some way to solving this problem by issuing a list of banned classes of drugs, though not a list of the drugs themselves, which would contain literally thousands of entries. An example of a banned class of drug is the androgenic anabolic steroids. The IOC then gives examples, i.e. testosterone. Even then, it is not possible to list every example, so a rider is included – 'and related compounds' – which covers all similar drugs.

The responsibility for checking whether a drug is banned or not rests squarely with the athlete. The information on banned classes and examples should be provided by the sports governing bodies. It is, in any case, available from the Sports Councils. The athlete needs to be sure that a drug is allowed before taking it.

Doping classes

Stimulants
Stimulants include drugs which increase alertness, reduce fatigue and may increase competitiveness and hostility.

Doping classes
Stimulants
Narcotics
Anabolic agents
Diuretics
Peptide hormones and analogues

Doping methods
Blood doping
Pharmacological, chemical and physical manipulation

Classes of drugs subject to certain restrictions
Alcohol
Marijuana
Local anaesthetics
Corticosteroids
Beta blockers

Their use can also produce loss of judgement, which may lead to accidents to the athletes themselves or to others. Amphetamine and related compounds have the most notorious reputation. Some deaths of sportsmen have resulted even when normal doses have been used under conditions of maximum physical activity. There is no medical reason for the use of amphetamines in sport.

One group of stimulants is the sympathomimetic amines, of which ephedrine is an example. In high doses, this type of compound produces mental stimulation and increased blood flow. Adverse effects include high blood pressure and headache, increased and irregular heartbeat, anxiety and tremor. In lower doses, they are often in cold and hay fever preparations, which can be bought in pharmacies and sometimes other retail outlets without a medical prescription.

Beta 2 agonists
The choice of medication to treat asthma and respiratory ailments has posed many problems. Some years ago, ephedrine and related substances were taken quite often. However, these substances are banned because they are classed as 'sympathomimetic amines' and therefore considered as stimulants.

Narcotic analgesics
The drugs in this class act specifically to control moderate to severe pain. This does not imply that their clinical effect is limited to the relief of trivial ailments. Most of these drugs have major side-effects, including dose-related respiratory depression, and carry a high risk of physical and psychological dependence. Evidence exists that narcotic analgesics have been and are abused in sports.

Anabolic agents
The androgenic anabolic steroids (AAS) class includes testosterone and related substances. They have been misused by the sports world to increase muscle strength and bulk, and to promote aggression. The use of AAS is associated with adverse effects on the liver, skin, cardiovascular and endocrine systems. They can promote the growth of tumours and induce psychiatric syndromes. In males, use of AAS can decrease the size of the testes and diminish sperm production. Females experience masculinisation, loss of breast tissue and diminished menstruation. The use of AAS by teenagers can stunt growth.

Diuretics
Diuretics have important properties for eliminating fluids from tissues, but strict medical control is needed. Diuretics are sometimes misused by competitors for two main reasons, namely: to lose weight quickly in sports where weight categories are involved and to reduce the concentration of drugs in urine by producing more rapid excretion to cut the risk of detection. Rapid loss of weight in sport cannot be justified medically, and serious side-effects may occur.

Methods

Blood doping

Blood doping is the giving of blood or related red blood products to an athlete other than for legitimate medical treatment.

This practice goes against the ethics of medicine and sport. There are also risks involved in the transfusion of blood and related blood products. These include the development of allergic reactions (rash, fever, etc) and acute haemolytic reaction, with kidney damage if incorrectly typed blood is used, as well as delayed transfusion reaction resulting in fever and jaundice, transmission of infectious diseases (viral hepatitis and HIV) and metabolic shock.

Pharmacological, chemical and physical manipulation

The IOC Medical Commission bans the use of substances and methods which alter the integrity and validity of urine samples used in doping control. Examples of banned methods are catheterisation, urine substitution and/or tampering and inhibition of renal excretion.

Classes of drugs subject to certain restrictions

Alcohol

Alcohol is not banned but breath or blood alcohol levels may be measured at the request of an International Federation, particularly in motorised sports.

Marijuana

Marijuana is not banned but tests may be carried out at the request of an International Federation.

Local anaesthetics

Injectable local anaesthetics are permitted only under certain conditions.

Cortico-steroids

The naturally occurring and synthetic corticosteroids are mainly used as anti-inflammatory drugs which also relieve pain. They produce euphoria and side-effects and therefore need medical control. Since 1975, the IOC Medical Commission has tried to restrict their use during competition by requiring a declaration from team doctors, but

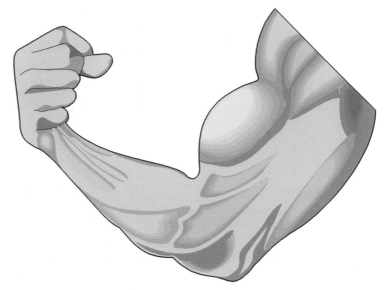

Anabolic steroids have been misused by the sports world to increase muscle strength and bulk

lately, stronger measures designed not to interfere with the appropriate medical use of these compounds have been introduced.

Beta blockers

The IOC Medical Commission has reviewed the therapeutic uses of beta blocking drugs and has found that there is now a wide range of effective alternatives to control hypertension, cardiac arrhythmias, angina pectoris and migraine. Due to the continued misuse of beta blockers in some sports where physical activity is of little or no importance, the IOC Medical Commission reserves the right to carry out tests as it sees fit. These are unlikely to cover endurance events which demand prolonged periods of high cardiac output and in which beta blockers would severely decrease performance.

Penalties

The penalties recommended by the IOC Medical Commission are as follows:

(a) Androgenic anabolic steroids, amphetamine-related and other stimulants, caffeine, diuretics, beta blockers, narcotic analgesics and designer drugs:
● two years for the first offence
● life ban for the second offence

(b) Ephedrine, phenylpropanolamine, etc (when taken orally as a cough suppressant or painkiller along with decongestants and/or antihistamines):

● a maximum three months for the first offence
● two years for the second offence
● life ban for the third offence

The IOC Medical Commission recommends that, before a final decision is made in each case, a fair hearing is given to the athlete. This hearing should consider the circumstances and the known facts of the case.

And finally!

● The IOC list is based on doping classes and methods with not all substances belonging to the class being listed. The fact that a substance is not listed does not mean it is not banned. The list of banned classes is updated regularly.
● Different sporting organisations may ban different drugs.

Banned substances are found not only in medicines prescribed by doctors. They may be found in over-the-counter preparations.

Medications from overseas should not be used unless they have been cleared with the governing body medical officer.

Some so-called 'vitamin' preparations and nutritional supplements may contain banned substances.

● The above is an extract from the information booklet *Doping in sport.*

© *The Sports Council for Wales*

How the problem of drugs has made itself felt in sports

Football

Soccer's testing programme has thrown up a number of high-profile cases of drug taking. Diego Maradona tested positive for cocaine in March 1991 and was banned for 15 months. This year he was thrown out of the World Cup after taking five different forms of the stimulant ephedrine to help with a weight loss programme.

His Argentinian international colleague, Claudio Caniggia, was banned in 1992 for 13 months following a positive test for cocaine.

In this country, the Football Association started drug testing in 1979. Since 1991, there have been four stimulant findings – three of them in Wales – including one positive test for amphetamines.

Golf

Mac O'Grady, former US tour player and coach to Seve Ballesteros, earlier this year accused seven of the world's top 30 players of taking beta blockers.

The drug, used in the treatment of heart complaints, suppresses adrenalin flows and could help players cope with the pressure of putting, he claimed.

Nick Price, winner of this year's Open, later admitted he had taken beta blockers for a congenital heart complaint but gave them up after they had an adverse effect on his game.

In July, former USPGA winner John Daly claimed some golfers on the US tour took cocaine but withdrew the allegation after he was criticised by his fellow professionals.

Rugby

Richie Griffiths, the former Wales B Rugby Union centre, became the first player in the world to be banned when he tested positive for anabolic steroids after a match in which he scored a try.

Lawrence Donegan

In Rugby League, Bradford Northern player Simon Tuffs was banned for two years after traces of amphetamine were found in his urine sample.

Since 1991, four players have tested positive for a range of drugs, including the analgesic dihydrocodeine which helps participants extend painful training sessions.

Snooker

Canadian player Kirk Stevens admitted taking cocaine in the late 1980s, but no action was taken by the sport's governing body as his drug-taking did not take place during competition.

Stevens' countryman, Bill Werbeniuk, was fined £2,000 and suspended in 1988 after he admitted taking the beta-blocker Inderal. He

suffered from a tremor in his cueing arm, and claimed he needed to consume copious amounts of lager to control the tremor and that Inderal was necessary to control the stress on his heart caused by his drinking.

Racing

Dope testing has long been a feature of racing and has uncovered a number of instances of fancied horses being 'stopped', usually by sedatives such as detomodine.

From October 1, jockeys will be subject to the same degree of scrutiny with random testing for a range of narcotics, including cannabis, cocaine, alcohol (above the legal limit for driving), and LSD. However, the list does not include the stimulant ephedrine or diuretics – known in the trade as 'pee pills' – which help overweight riders to shed precious pounds.

Other sports

The taking of banned substances is not the preserve of highly paid athletes, as the recent case of a 73 year old Scottish grandmother illustrated. She was forced to pull out of this year's Scottish national bowling championships because tablets she was prescribed after a heart bypass were on the sport's list of banned sub-stances.

A Sports Council report published earlier this year reveals that drug abuse takes place in a wide range of sports: beta blockers in archery; steroids in cycling; painkillers in boxing; even netball has thrown up two positive tests for banned stimulants.

More predictably, 44 power lifters tested positive for steroids in the last six years, while there have been six cases of cannabis abuse in surfing.

© The Guardian
August, 1994

INDEX

ADDITIONAL RESOURCES

You might like to contact the following organisations for further information. Due to the increasing cost of postage, many organisations cannot respond to inquiries unless they receive a stamped, addressed envelope.

For information relating to a specific sport, you may want to contact the relevant governing body. The Sports Councils in England, Scotland and Wales each provide governing body contacts for their regions. See below for Sports Councils address details.

ISDD (Institute for the Study of Drug Dependence))
Waterbridge House
32-36 Loman Street
London SE1 0EE
Tel: 0171 928 1211

Provides books, leaflets and other information. The ISDD has the largest drugs reference library in Europe.

Lifeline
101-103 Oldham Street
Manchester M5 4AQ
Tel: 0161 839 2054

Provides advice, information and help for young drug users and their parents.

Professional Footballers Association
2 Oxford Court
Bishop's Gate
Manchester
M2 3WQ
Tel: 0161 236 0575

SCODA (Standing body on drug abuse)
Waterbridge House
32-36 Loman Street
London SE1 0EE
Tel: 0171 928 9500

Provides up to the minute advice with details of regional bodies. In the event of you, or a colleague or any member of your family are faced with a drug problem, SCODA will give you the details of the nearest and most appropriate agency in your region to offer advice or assistance.

Sir Norman Chester Centre for Football Research
Dept. of Sociology
University of Leicester
University Road
Leicester
LE1 7RH
Tel: 01162 522741

Has a series of free fact sheets on sport-related issues including hooliganism, racism and women in sport

Sports Council Doping Control Unit
Walkden House
3-10 Melton Street
London
NW1 2EB
Tel: 0171 383 5667

Has a wide range of leaflets and books on drugs in sport such as their *Drugs Information Pack*. Ask for their publications list.

TACADE (The Advisory Council on Alcohol & Drug Education)
1 Hulme Place
The Crescent
Salford
Manchester M5 4QA
Tel: 0161 745 8925

Drugs education resources and training for schools, youth service, professionals, parents and carers. They also publish A *Factual Guide to Drugs in Sport*.

The Football Association
Medical Education Centre
Lilleshall Hall National Sports Centre
near Newport
Shropshire
TF10 9AT
Tel: 01952 605928
Fax: 01952 825 496

Provides information on illegal drugs in football.

The Football Trust
Walkden House
10 Melton Street
London NW1 2EJ
Tel: 0171 388 4504
Fax: 0171 388 6688

The Scottish Sports Council
Caledonia House
South Gyle
Edinburgh
EH12 9D
Tel: 0131 317 7200
Fax: 0131 317 7200

Has a wide range of leaflets and books on sport-related issues. Ask for their publications list.

The Sports Council
16 Upper Woburn Place
London
WC1H 0QP
Tel: 0171 388 1277
Fax: 0171 383 5740

Has a wide range of leaflets and books on sport-related issues. Ask for their publications list.

The Sports Council for Wales
Sophia Gardens
Cardiff
South Glamorgan CF1 9SW
Tel: 0171 388 1277
Fax: 0171 383 5740

Has a wide range of leaflets and books on sport-related issues. Ask for their publications list.

ACKNOWLEDGEMENTS

The publisher is grateful for permission to reproduce the following material

Chapter One: Hooliganism in sport

Football and hooligans, © Sir Norman Chester Centre for Football Research, *It's back - terror on the terraces*, © The Northern Echo, February 1995, *Fan's death leaves national game in mourning again*, © The Telegraph Plc, London 1995, *A whole new ball game*, © The Guardian, May 1995, *Courts told to be hard on soccer hooligans*, © The Telegraph Plc, London 1995, *Time to combat fascist threat*, © The Independent, March 1995, *Fair play – the winning way*, © The Council of Europe, March 1995, *The worst attack I've ever seen in football*, © The Evening Standard, January 1995, *Springboks code of dishonour*, © The Daily Mail, June 1995, *Writing on the wall for thugs*, © Today, July 1994, *Time to blow whistle on beast within*, © The Independent, September 1995, *Security top priority for Euro matches*, © Nottingham Evening Post, March 1995, *Tragic wish of boxer who put his life on the line for £8,000*, © The Daily Mirror, April 1994, *Box on*, © The Daily Mirror, April 1995, *Ban it*, © The Daily Mirror, April 1995,

Chapter Two: Drugs in sport

Why some athletes take drugs, © The Sports Council for Wales, *Drugs in sport*, © The Sports Council, May 1995, *Doping control in sport*, © The Sports Council, March 1989, *I just wanted to get to the top*, © The Independent, October 1994, *Haunted by the past*, © The Independent, October 1994, *Today's shame was born from sins of the past*, © The Sunday Times, Au... History of doping in modern sport, © The Sp... March 1989, *Athletes sanctioned for posit... during Olympic Games*, © Interna... Committee (IOC), *Test statistics re... -ridden sport'*, © The Independent... *This sporting strife*, © The Guardian, ... *...hy I will carry on taking steroids*, © ... ...rch 1995, *Testing procedures*, © The Spor... Council, *UK legislation on doping substances ir...* ... The Sports Council *Doping Control* ... *...ed?*, © The Sports Council for W... ...m of drugs has made itself felt ir... ...dian, August 1994.

... and Illustrations

P... ...w Smith/Folio Collective, pages 4, ...odd/Folio Collective, page 5: Sean ... ...ress Association, page 6: Anthony ... ...ornthwaite/Folio Collective, page 13: Adam butler/Press Association, pages 14, 24, 34: Ken Pyne, page 15: David Jones/Press Association, pages 21, 22, 33: Chris Taylor/The Sports Council, page 29: Deutshe Presse – Agentur GMBH/Press Association.

Craig Donnellan
Cambridge
September, 1995